WITHDRAWN
UTSA Libraries

RENEWALS 458-4574
DATE DUE

Magic Numbers for Bonds and Derivatives

How to Calculate 25 Key Ratios for Investing Success

Magic Numbers for Bonds and Derivatives

How to Calculate 25 Key Ratios for Investing Success

Peter Temple

John Wiley & Sons (Asia) Pte Ltd

Copyright © 2005 by John Wiley & Sons (Asia) Pte Ltd
Published in 2005 by John Wiley & Sons (Asia) Pte Ltd
2 Clementi Loop, #02-01, Singapore 129809

Peter Temple has asserted his right, under the 1988 Copyright Design and Patent Act 1988, to be identified as the author of this work.

All rights reserved.

No part of this publication may be reproduced, stored in a retrieval system or transmitted in any form or by any means, electronic, mechanical, photocopying, recording, scanning or otherwise, except as expressly permitted by law, without either the prior written permission of the Publisher, or authorization through payment of the appropriate photocopy fee to the Copyright Clearance Center. Requests for permission should be addressed to the Publisher, John Wiley & Sons (Asia) Pte Ltd, 2 Clementi Loop, #02-01, Singapore 129809, tel: 65-64632400, fax: 65-64646912, e-mail: enquiry@wiley.com.sg.

This publication is designed to provide accurate and authoritative information in regard to the subject matter covered. It is sold with the understanding that the publisher is not engaged in rendering professional services. If professional advice or other expert assistance is required, the services of a competent professional person should be sought.

Other Wiley Editorial Offices

John Wiley & Sons, 111 River Street, Hoboken, NJ 07030, USA
John Wiley & Sons, The Atrium Southern Gate, Chichester P019 8SQ, England
John Wiley & Sons (Canada) Ltd, 22 Worcester Road, Rexdale, Ontario M9W 1L1, Canada
John Wiley & Sons Australia Ltd, 33 Park Road (PO Box 1226), Milton, Queensland 4064, Australia
Wiley-VCH, Pappellaee 3, 69469 Weinheim, Germany

Library of Congress Cataloging-in-Publication Data

0-470-82139-6 (cloth)

Typeset in 12/14 points, Times Roman by Cepha Imaging Pvt. Ltd.
Printed in Singapore by Saik Wah Press Ltd
10 9 8 7 6 5 4 3 2

Contents

Acknowledgments   vii

Introduction   ix

Part One: Bond "Magic Numbers" – Basics   1
1. Compounding   7
2. Discounting   12
3. Accrued interest   18
4. Running yield   25
5. Redemption yield   31
6. Yield on a zero-coupon bond   37
7. Yield to worst   44
8. Redemption yield on an index-linked bond   50

Part Two: Bond "Magic Numbers" – Analysis   59
9. Yield spreads   63
10. Yield curve   68
11. Duration   75
12. Macaulay duration   81
13. Basis-point value   87
14. Convexity and convexity adjustment   92

Part Three: Futures and Options "Magic Numbers"   101
15. Volatility   105
16. Fair value of a future   110
17. Fair value of an option   116
18. Time value and intrinsic value of an option   125
19. Delta and gamma   130
20. Vega, rho and theta   138
21. Returns on covered call writing   145
22. The put–call ratio   154

Part Four: Convertibles and Warrants "Magic Numbers" **159**
23 Convertible bonds – conversion premium and payback 163
24 Breakeven rate and capital fulcrum point 169
25 Covered warrant gearing 175

Appendix: Finding the information 181

Index **193**

Acknowledgments

Thanks to...

Nick Wallwork, my publisher at Wiley Asia, for sparking the original idea for the "magic numbers" series and turning it into profitable reality.

Janis Soo, my editor at Wiley Asia, for shepherding the book to publication.

John Owen for copy-editing, proofreading and his observations on content.

Lynn Temple, for her commentary on the book's content, for checking for errors at final proof stage, for researching and writing the appendix, and for compiling the index.

Introduction

"Magic Numbers" for Bonds and Derivatives – The Basics

In the original *Magic Numbers* book and in *Magic Numbers for Stock Investors*, I looked at how to calculate some simple accounting ratios. Those "magic numbers" were designed to make it easy to evaluate whether or not to buy a particular company's shares.

This book is slightly different. It looks at other investments with which some investors may be less familiar. These are bonds; so-called derivatives, such as futures, options and warrants; and hybrids of the two, such as convertible bonds.

Securities like this used to be the preserve of professionals. But it is now much easier for private investors to use them. To use bonds and derivatives effectively, however, you need to understand the concepts behind them.

But it's not all "rocket science". As with company investing, there are some easy ways you can evaluate them. Some of the concepts and calculations that we are going to meet are more complex than those connected with straightforward share investment, but many of them are simple common sense. There is also a pleasing precision about many of the concepts. Often decisions about investing in bonds and derivatives are quite clear-cut, without the interpretation that may be necessary when dealing with company accounts and share investing.

As before, *Magic Numbers for Bonds and Derivatives* strips away the jargon and uses simple examples from real-life financial markets. It shows you how to calculate 25 key ratios that really matter when valuing bonds, a financial future, an option or a warrant.

You don't need to be an accountant or a PhD in mathematics to read this book, and any specialist terminology we use will be explained in easy-to-understand terms. One interesting aspect of bonds and derivatives such as futures and options is that the ways in which they are valued is universal. There are few, if any, differences in the way in which investors go about assessing bonds issued in the UK, the USA, Singapore or Japan. Similarly, valuing a future or an option listed on SGX or TIFFE is the same as valuing one listed on London's LIFFE or Chicago's CBOT.

As with the previous two books in the *Magic Numbers* series, all you will need is a basic grasp of how numbers and arithmetic work. You also need an enquiring mind, and the ability to use a calculator, simple computer software, and some of the online resources that allow the more complex calculations to be done with the minimum of fuss.

"Magic Numbers", Bond Markets, and Financial Futures and Options

The "magic numbers" in this book will help you understand and evaluate bonds, futures, options and warrants as investment propositions in their own right, and relative to their peers.

Whether a share is undervalued or overvalued can often be worked out by looking at the share price. It is an indicator of the value assigned by the stock market to the company and what the accountants would say is behind its underlying value – its profits, cash flow and assets.

Comparing the market's view with the objective numbers the accountants have produced helps you work out whether a share is cheap or expensive, or somewhere in between.

In the case of a bond or derivative, the valuation criteria are a little different. For bonds, often what they are indicating is the likely return you will earn and measuring this against the risk you will run in holding it.

In the case of some measures relating to derivatives, for example, the "magic numbers" in question will allow us to work out the potential profit from buying or selling an option under certain pre-set assumptions.

Unlike the "magic numbers" for stock investors, however, the ratios outlined in this book can't all be worked out using a simple pocket calculator. Some require you to use a financial calculator. I use the Texas Instruments BAII Plus. This is relatively easy to use. You need a financial calculator that allows you to calculate bond yields, compound growth rates and one or two other basic financial parameters. Other "magic numbers" may require you to use simple computer software or online calculators.

Wherever possible we will keep the calculation as simple as possible. If we use online calculators or software, we will indicate where you can get them. We will try to ensure wherever possible that these tools are free to use.

A considerable amount of information on bonds and derivatives can also be found from the financial pages of leading daily newspapers and from the websites of stock exchanges and derivatives markets around the world.

But don't take the "magic numbers" provided by web- or print-based sources as being entirely reliable. There is no substitute, for calculating the "magic numbers" yourself. It will give you an insight into the way the bond or derivative functions, which is valuable in itself.

There are several useful web addresses in the appendix at the end of the book.

How this Book is Organized

We've grouped each set of "magic number" sections into a logical sequence. They look in turn at:

- basics of bond yields and how to calculate and interpret them, both for conventional bonds and some other common types

- other analytical concepts relevant to bond investing
- basic concepts underlying futures and options, and calculating their value
- basic concepts underlying convertibles and warrants, and calculating their value.

Each section contains an overview of the ratios and how they are used.

Each of the 25 "magic number" sections is organized in the same way.

They each contain:

- a definition of the "magic number" in words and symbols
- a definition of its components
- information on where to find the information needed to calculate it
- a theoretical example of how to calculate it
- an actual example of how to calculate it
- the significance of the "magic number" and how to interpret it.

WILL YOU USE THESE "MAGIC NUMBERS" MORE IN FUTURE?

The answer is "Yes". Sensible diversification means that more investors are looking to have bonds in their portfolio as well as stocks and to use derivatives to speculate and hedge. These "magic numbers" allow you to assess investments like this and to work out how they can be used to tailor the risks you run and the income you earn from your portfolio.

Knowing what the numbers mean can give you an investing edge.

Lack of uniformity in accounting means that interpreting the "magic numbers" for a stock can be complicated. With bonds and derivatives these differences are much less apparent. While there are some variations, in the main the language of bonds, and of futures and options and the like, is the same in whatever market you invest.

Read on to make a start on these interesting areas of the investment scene.

Part One
Bond "Magic Numbers" – Basics

Bond "Magic Numbers" – Basics

Each of the eight "magic numbers" in this section is a basic building block for evaluating bonds. All of them are either ways to calculate the return on different types of bond, or concepts that you need to master in order to understand how to calculate them. If you expect bonds to be one of your main areas of interest in the future, reading this section alone should help you grasp what bond investing is all about.

Most investors who have so far confined their trading to buying and selling stocks may have some understanding of what bonds are, but let's just give a brief and exact explanation at the outset.

Bonds are loans that trade on the stock market. Governments issue them, as do quasi-government entities such as cities and municipalities, and companies.

Most conventional bonds have a fixed interest rate (or coupon) paid either once or twice yearly, and a fixed date and price – generally 100% of their nominal face value – at which they will be redeemed (that is, repaid) and capital returned to the holder. You could pay $1,600, or $1,400, for a bond with a face value of $1,500. Whatever you pay, $1,500 is what you will get if you hold the bond until it is redeemed.

The return on a bond primarily depends on the interest rate it pays and the difference between the price you pay and the price at which it will be redeemed in the future. You do not necessarily have to hold it until it is redeemed. But if you do, then your return can be precisely forecast at the outset.

This means that bonds, particularly those of high-quality issuers, such as G7 governments and big listed companies, tend to be more predictable investments than shares. This predictability normally means lower returns for investors. While this may seem to mark them out as inferior, this is not the case. Bonds give balance to a portfolio. Mix riskier shares with lower-risk bonds and you should get more stable returns. One old market saying is that the percentage of bonds in your portfolio should roughly equal your age in years.

There will be more explanation about how bonds work as we go through the different "magic number" sections. In brief, the concepts we are going to cover are:

- compounding and discounting – these are the basic mathematical concepts central to bond investing.

- accrued interest – understanding accrued interest and how to calculate it is also an important part of bond investing, because it affects the way in which bond prices are expressed.

- running yield – the simplest of all the ways of calculating the return on a bond.

- redemption yields – the most accurate way of comparing different bonds and take into account several other variables not used in calculating running yield. These include income from reinvesting coupons received during the bond's life; the length of the bond's remaining life; and the capital gain or loss implied by the difference between price you pay and the redemption price.

- bonds that carry no coupon, with the whole of the return on the bond coming in the capital gain arising between the purchase price and the price at which the bond is eventually redeemed. Calculating this return is an important part of the bond investor's toolkit, but relatively easy to master.

- bonds that have provisions which allow the issuer the option of redeeming the bond early at a pre-set price. These need to be assessed slightly differently.

- bonds with interest payments and the repayment of principal linked to a measure of inflation such as the UK's RPI or the US's CPI. Knowing how to calculate the yield on an index-linked bond is important.

All of these "magic numbers" are absolutely basic to bond investing. If you become an active bond investor you will find you use them constantly to assess the merits of different bonds and to time when you buy and sell them.

The sections that follow examine each of these eight "magic numbers" in more detail. Read on to find out how to get the data you need, how to calculate them, and what they mean.

A word of warning at the outset. Don't be put off by the algebraic formulas used here and there, or what seem to be complex examples. It is often the case that a financial calculator or computer spreadsheet, or an online calculator, will do the work for you. The formulas and examples are there to help you understand the basics.

MAGIC NUMBER 1

Compounding

THE DEFINITION

Compounding and discounting are fundamental to bond investing. This is why they are the first two "magic numbers" in the book. You need to grasp these ideas before we go on to look at some other concepts.

Compounding is based on the principle of earning interest-on-interest. Lend $1,000 at 10% and at the end of year one you receive $100 interest. Assuming you can lend out the interest you receive at the same rate, you can then earn interest at 10% on $1,100 ($1,000 you started with, plus the $100 interest you received). At the end of year two you receive interest of $110 (10% of $1,100). You now have $1,210 to lend out at 10%. At the end of year three you receive interest of $121. You now have $1,331 to lend out, and so on. Calculating compound interest requires you to assume an initial investment (the principal) and an annual rate of interest.

THE FORMULA

For compound interest, the future value (FV) – the original investment with compounded interest added – can be worked out using the following formula:

$$FV = P \times (1 + R)^n$$

In this formula, P is the principal (your initial investment), R is the annual rate of interest expressed as a decimal, and n is the number of years over which the interest will be compounded.

For working out compounding for a bond that pays interest twice yearly, the formula becomes:

$$FV = P \times (1 + R/2)^{2n}$$

In other words, the interest part of the equation is expressed as half the original rate but raised to the power that corresponds to the number of coupon periods, rather than the number of years of interest earned. This is an important distinction. Where an interest payment is received part way through the year, it can begin earning interest-on-interest immediately. Because of this, its value when compounding is higher.

The Components

Compound interest calculations have three simple variables: principal, rate of interest and time periods.

Principal – this is simply the original money amount invested, in this case in a bond.

Rate of interest – this is the annual or periodic interest received. In the case of most bonds, interest is usually paid either once a year or twice yearly (semi-annually). It is worth remembering that the effective interest rate on a bond corresponds to the coupon only if the bond is purchased at 100% of its nominal (or face) value.

Time periods – this is the number of periods over which interest is earned. In the case of a bond that pays interest annually, this could be a number of years. Or, in the case of a bond that pays interest more than once a year, it could be a number of coupon payments. A bond with exactly 10 years to run that pays interest twice yearly will have 20 coupon periods. The last coupon period will correspond to the bond's redemption date, when the principal, in the form of the face value of the bond, will also be returned with the last interest payment.

Where's the Data?

Principal – this is self-explanatory. It is your initial investment.

Rate of interest – this is the interest on a loan or a deposit account, or the coupon rate on a bond purchased at par (that is, exactly 100% of its nominal value). If you buy a bond at a price other than par, the coupon rate multiplied by 100 divided by the price paid gives the actual rate earned. For example, a 5% coupon purchased at 95 equates to a compounding rate of interest of 5 × 100/95, or 5.263%.

Time periods – the number of intervals during which interest is paid. This will correspond to the remaining number of years, if interest is paid annually. In the case of a bond that pays interest twice yearly, there will be either one or two payments in the current year, then two payments each year for the remaining years of the bond's life. This needs to be worked out with care in each case.

CALCULATING IT – THE THEORY

Figure 1.1 shows the different numbers to be pulled from the sources described and how to use them to calculate the ratio.

Figure 1.1 Calculating the "Magic Number" for... Compound Interest

The Bank of Pluto offers a high-interest account that pays interest at 5% a year. Interest is paid at the end of each year. You deposit $10,000 in the account. What is your balance at the end of five years?

The formula is: $FV = P \times (1 + R)^n$

$P = \$10,000$
$R = 0.05$ (ie 5%)
$n = 5$

The formula becomes: FV = 10,000 × (1.05 to the power 5)
                        FV = 10,000 × 1.276
                        FV = 12,760

As a check, principal plus interest at the end of each year on $10,000 @ 5% interest is shown below:

Year 1   10,000 × 1.05 = 10,500
Year 2   10,500 × 1.05 = 11,025
Year 3   11,025 × 1.05 = 11,576
Year 4   11,576 × 1.05 = 12,155
Year 5   12,155 × 1.05 = 12,762 or approximately 12,760 allowing for rounding.

Calculating it for
UK TREASURY

Figure 1.2 Calculating Compound Interest for UK Treasury 5% 2008

The figures ...

The UK Treasury 5% stock 2008 pays interest on 7th March and 7th September and is repaid at 100 on 7th March, 2008.

You invest £10,000 in the stock on 8th March, 2004, at a price of 102.

Calculate the compound interest element in your return if you hold the bond to maturity.

The calculation ...

The formula is: $FV = P \times (1+R/2)^{2n}$

P = £10,000
R = 0.05 × 100/102 = 0.049

The effective rate of interest earned is the coupon rate of 5% adjusted for the price you paid.

R/2 = 0.0245
n = 4 (years to maturity)
2n = 8 (number of coupon periods to maturity)

The formula becomes: FV = 10,000 × (1.0245 to the power 8)
                       FV = 10,000 × 1.214
                       FV = 12,140

The compound interest element in your return is £2,140 (12,140–10,000)
In other words, the effective annual rate is 0.214 × 100/4 years, or 5.35% per year.

As a check, principal plus interest at the end of each coupon period on £10,000 @ 2.45% interest is shown

Period 1   10,000 × 1.0245 = 10,245
Period 2   10,245 × 1.0245 = 10,496
Period 3   10,496 × 1.0245 = 10,753
Period 4   10,753 × 1.0245 = 11,016
Period 5   11,016 × 1.0245 = 11,286
Period 6   11,286 × 1.0245 = 11,563
Period 7   11,563 × 1.0245 = 11,846
Period 8   11,846 × 1.0245 = 12,136 or 12,140 allowing for rounding.

WHAT IT MEANS

Compound interest is one of the wonders of the world. Many stock investors often overlook its importance, even though they may hold investments that work on this principle – whether it is having dividend income from a unit trust or mutual fund reinvested, or through owning a bond and reinvesting the interest they receive from it.

The real power of compounding is rarely fully appreciated. Modest annual returns of 7% will compound to more or less double your capital in 10 years. A more generous 10% annual return will accomplish the same feat in seven years.

Benefiting from compounding means having the discipline not to spend investment income but to reinvest it. For many investors this may not be possible because some rely on income from investments to supplement their earnings or pensions. It also assumes that the investor is able to reinvest interest or dividend at the same rate at which it was earned, which may not always be the case if interest rates or bond yields are changing.

Either way, taking advantage of compounding remains an option for investors, whether or not they make use of it. And assuming reinvestment can be accomplished at the same rate of interest is a better assumption than ignoring this aspect completely. The phenomenon of interest-on-interest is one of the central pillars of returns from bonds and we cannot ignore it.

MAG1C NUM8ER 2

Discounting

THE DEFINITION

Discounting is compounding in reverse. It attempts to work out the value today of an amount received in the future when adjusted for a particular rate of change. (This is known as the "time value of money" theory and is touched on again in Magic Number 10.)

One way of visualizing this is by relating it to price inflation. Let's say you are due to receive $1,000 in a year's time, the same amount in two years' time and again in three years' time. But annual inflation is expected to be 10% for each of the next three years.

The $1,000 you receive in a year's time only has the purchasing power of $900 today. In two years' time, the $1,000 you receive then will only be worth $810 in today's money. And in three years' time, the $1,000 will only be worth $729 in terms of its present value. In other words, you are *discounting* your future payments at 10% a year to get to their true value in today's spending power when you receive them.

The elements required to calculate this discounted value are a future receipt or series of receipts, an annual discount rate, and a time period over which the discounting takes place.

THE FORMULA

In discounting, the present value (PV) – the future value discounted back to today's money – can be worked out using the following formula:

$$PV = FV \times (1 - D)^n$$

In this formula, FV is the payment that you expect to receive at some point in the future, D is the discount rate expressed as a decimal, and n is the number of years in the future that the future value will be received.

In the example given in the section above, taking the part where we discounted $1,000 at 10% for three years, the formula becomes $PV = 1,000 \times (0.9)^3$.

Using a calculator, we can easily work out that the figure 0.9 to the power 3 ($0.9 \times 0.9 \times 0.9$) is 0.729 which, when multiplied by $1,000, gives the answer we asserted on the previous page.

In fact, if you look back at Magic Number 1, it becomes obvious that discounting is really the mirror image of compounding. In compounding, we are adding at a given rate to a present value to arrive at a future value. In discounting, we are subtracting at a given rate from a future value to arrive at a present value.

THE COMPONENTS

Future value – you normally use discounting to work out the present value of a series of cash flows. Those who read the original *Magic Numbers* and *Magic Numbers for Stock Investors* will remember that one "magic number" we described there was discounted cash flow for a company. This added up the discounted future cash flows for a period of years to arrive at a supposed present value for the company's shares.

With a bond, we can fix cash flows with much greater precision than this. We know the timing and size of a bond's cash flows in advance. They are the regular coupon payments, interest-on-interest, and the return of principal at maturity. Each of these can be discounted back to arrive at the present value of the stream of cash the bond represents.

Discount rate – the choice of a discount rate in circumstances like this is academic. In fact, the way discounting is applied to bonds is in calculating redemption yield (see Magic Number 5) and duration (see Magic Number 11).

In the case of redemption yield, for example, we start out with the bond's flows of cash out into the future, and its present value as expressed by its "dirty" price (that is, its price including accrued interest – see Magic Number 3). The redemption yield is the annual discount rate that equates one to the other.

WHERE'S THE DATA?

Future value – for the purposes of discounting, a schedule of future values needs to be worked out in terms of time and amount. In the case of a bond, this will be apparent from a bond's terms, which will supply coupon rate, payment frequency and maturity date (when the principal amount is returned along with the final coupon payment). A bond's terms, obtainable from a newspaper, a prospectus or a financial website will provide the necessary information.

Discount rate – in redemption yield calculations, discount rate is the rate that equates "dirty price" to the discounted flows of coupons and principal repayment. In duration calculations – calculations of the bond's true "half-life" – the discount rate used is the bond's own redemption yield.

Other discount rates that can potentially be used in calculations like this are the risk-free rate of return, which is the redemption yield on a government bond of identical maturity, or the expected yield on a bond in the future, which can be used to project the likely price movement in a bond from today's price. It is this latter use that we will look at in the examples below.

This may seem complicated, but all should become clear.

DISCOUNTING

Figure 2.1 Calculating the "Magic Number" for ... Discounting

Problem

The Bank of Saturn 5% 2008 pays interest annually and matures on 31st December, 2008. It is now 1st January, 2005 and the bond is priced at 100. You have invested $1,000. You think interest rates will fall to 4% quickly, causing the bond price to rise. What is the potential price appreciation in the bond in the short term?

Solution

Work out the future cash flows in the bond and discount them at 4% pa. Compare the result with the current price of 100 and your investment of $1,000.

The schedule of cash flows looks like this:

Date	Type	Amount	Discount	Value
31.12.05	Coupon	$50	discounted @ 4% for one year	48.08
Working				(50/1.08)
31.12.06	Coupon	$50	discounted @ 4% for two years	46.22
Working				(50/1.08^2)
31.12.07	Coupon	$50	discounted @ 4% for three years	44.44
Working				(50/1.08^3)
31.12.08	C+Principal	$1,050	discounted @ 4% for four years	897.54
Working				(50/1.08^4)
Total of discounted cash flows				$1,036.28

In other words, a move in yields from the present 5% to 4% will produce a rise in the value of the investment from $1,000 to 1,030.13. This equates to a rise in price from 100 to 103.13.

Calculating it for
CHINA DEVELOPMENT BANK

Figure 2.2 Calculating Discount Rate implications for China Development Bank 8.25% Eurobond 2009

The figures ...

Problem

The China Development Bank Eurodollar bond 8.25% 2009 pays interest annually. It matures on 15th May, 2009. It is now 16th May, 2005 and the bond is priced at 121.8. You have invested $10,000.

You think the yield basis on the bond will rise from its current 3.5% to around 5%. What is the potential downward movement in the price if this happens?

Solution

Work out the future cash flows on the bond and discount them at 5% pa. Compare the result with the value of your investment of $10,000.

Rate earned on bond adjusted for purchase price is 6.77%
(working)   (8.25 × 100/121.8)

Your annual coupon is therefore worth $677
(working)   (10,000 × 0.0677)

Your return of capital on maturity will be $8,210
(working)   (10,000 × 100/121.8)

The calculation ...

Your schedule of cash flows looks like this:

Date	Type	Amount	Discount	Value
15.05.06	Coupon	$677	discounted @ 5% for one year	644.76
Working				(677/1.05)
15.05.07	Coupon	$677	discounted @ 5% for two years	614.06
Working				(677/1.05^2)
15.05.08	Coupon	$677	discounted @ 5% for three years	584.82
Working				(677/1.05^3)
15.05.09	C+Principal	$8,887	discounted @ 5% for four years	7,311.36
Working				(677/1.05^4)

Total of discounted cash flows $9,155.00

In other words, a move in yields from the present 3.5% to 5% will produce a fall in the value of the investment from $10,000 to $9,073. This equates to a fall in price from 121.8 to 110.5. The new price is calculated by multiplying the old price of 121.8 by 9,073/10,000.

WHAT IT MEANS

These examples represent some of the simplest ways discounting can be used in the bond market. Like compounding, the concept of discounting underpins many other aspects of the bond market, including the redemption yield on a bond, the return on a zero-coupon bond, and the calculation of a bond's duration.

Let's just stress one point. It is an understanding of the idea of discounting (and compounding, for that matter) that is important, rather than the mechanics of the calculation. More often than not, the calculations can be performed without much ado by a financial calculator or in a computer spreadsheet; but you need to understand why they work as they do, and how to apply them.

For the sake of presenting a clear example, we have ignored the complicating factor of interest-on-interest mentioned in the previous section, even though this is theoretically part of a bond's cash flow.

Even if a bond investor reinvests each successive interest payment as soon as it is received, the impact of interest-on-interest is generally relatively small in most discounting calculations. One reason for this is that the single most important component in the calculation is the discounting of the final interest payment and principal redemption value at the end of the bond's life.

Because this is the last element in the calculation, there is no interest-on-interest to be earned on this much larger total amount. And, as we will see later, discounting is particularly important for working out the return on zero-coupon bonds. In this case, because bonds like this pay no interest, there is no interest-on-interest element to worry about.

MAG1C NUM8ER 3

Accrued Interest

THE DEFINITION

Accrued interest (AI) is the interest that has been earned since the last interest payment date of a bond. When a bond is traded, the buyer pays this additional amount to the seller, on top of the normal market price, to compensate the seller for the loss of this interest when the next payment is made to the new owner of the bond.

THE FORMULA

AI in money terms = Coupon × (Trade settlement date − Last interest payment date)/365 × Face value of bond

AI in price terms = Coupon × (Trade settlement date − Last interest payment date)/365

In other words, the accrued interest in money terms is the coupon (expressed as a decimal) multiplied by the decimal fraction of a year that has elapsed since the last payment date, multiplied by the face value (sometimes called "nominal value") of the bond. When accrued interest is expressed in terms of the price of the bond, the nominal value is not relevant.

THE COMPONENTS

Coupon – the coupon is the fixed-percentage interest rate payable on the face value of the bond. A 5% bond with a face value (or par value, or nominal value) of £1,000 pays interest at the rate of £50 a year (5% of £1,000). Depending on where market prices sit at the time, you may have to pay more than the face value to acquire the bond, or be able to buy it for less. But interest will always be based on the face value of the stock you have bought. A bond is normally repaid at its face (or par, or nominal) value.

Trade date – the trade settlement date is one of the dates on which accrued interest is based. This is not necessarily the date your order is transacted. In most markets, settlement will be one to three days later. Government bonds often settle faster than shares. In the UK, gilts (British government bonds) settle on the basis of trade date plus three days (T + 3). US Treasury notes and bonds settle on the basis of T + 1.

Last interest payment date – interest payment dates on bonds vary. Some bonds pay interest once a year; others pay interest twice yearly. For the purposes of calculating accrued interest this should be borne in mind, since it is important for some conventions used in calculating accrued interest. In the event that there is an ex-dividend date, after which buyers lose the right to the old dividend for several days before the new dividend begins accruing, this needs to be taken into account as well.

Face value of bond – this is important for calculating the money amount of accrued interest. The face value of the bond and the price you pay for it will almost certainly differ. Face value is normally based on the price at a par value of 100. Let's say you invest €10,000 in a bond at a price of 101. Ignoring dealing costs for a moment, you will not actually be buying €10,000 in terms of face value. The face (or nominal) value of the bonds you buy will actually be 10,000 × 100/101, or €9,901. It is the latter figure that is the basis for the cash interest payments you receive and for accrued interest calculations.

Day-count convention – an added complication is that different assumptions are used to calculate accrued interest in different markets. You need to be familiar with the day-count convention used in your particular market to be able to calculate the appropriate level of accrued interest. Financial calculators do support most of the different day-count conventions.

Figure 3.1 below shows the common day-count bases for calculating accrued interest in different government bond markets.

Figure 3.1 Day-count Conventions for Government Bonds

Market	Coupon	Day-count basis	Ex-dividend period
Eurobonds	Annual	30/360	No
France	Annual	Actual/Actual	No
Germany	Annual	Actual/Actual	No
Switzerland	Annual	30E/360	No
UK	Semi-annual	Actual/Actual	Yes
USA	Semi-annual	Actual/Actual	No
Japan	Semi-annual	Actual/365	No

Note:
30/360 means every month (including February) is assumed to have 30 days; the year is assumed to be 360 days. Typically used for short-term debt such as Treasury bills and commercial paper.

Actual/actual means actual days counted are used for both numerator and denominator. Typically used for bonds with semiannual coupons.

Actual/365 is for actual/actual except that the extra day in leap years is ignored. 30E/360 is a slight variant of 30/360.

Ex-dividend period applies in the UK (also in Norway and Denmark) and is seven days in length.

These conventions are worth paying attention to because they each give slightly different results, as the following brief example shows.

Assume a bond with a 5% coupon, a coupon date of 1st February and a settlement date for the trade of 1st March. Under the actual/actual convention, the accrued interest amount would be 0.3836 ($28/365 \times 5\%$). Under the 30/360 convention, the accrued interest would be 0.4166 ($30/360 \times 5\%$). Not a big difference, but significant enough on a large trade.

In fact, the actual/actual convention is often used for bonds that pay interest on a semi-annual basis and the calculation is done on the six-monthly period in question rather than the full year. While this might seem pedantic, there is a reason for it. The six-month period that includes February, the shortest month, has fewer days than the one that does not. This does make a difference to accrued interest amounts.

Where's the Data?

Coupon – leading financial newspapers such as the *Wall Street Journal*, *Asian Wall Street Journal* and *Financial Times* have a section of their price pages devoted to bonds, especially government securities. The coupon is normally one of the first pieces of information stated with respect to a bond, along with its year of maturity.

Trade settlement date – trade settlement day varies from market to market, but is usually one to three days after the day your trade is executed. The settlement day is stated on the broker's contract note. For orders placed electronically, this will usually appear on the electronic dealing "ticket" prior to you confirming the details and executing the transaction.

Interest payment date – this requires hunting out. Most often, financial newspapers carry this information from time to time, perhaps on a weekly basis. Alternatively, the data can usually be obtained either from a broker or from the website of the issuer. In the UK, the Debt Management Office (www.dmo.gov.uk) has this information. In the US, the Public Debt Office of the US Treasury does the same.

Face value of the bonds you hold – this will be stated on the contract note when you buy them, or on the certificate you hold or receive following a purchase.

Day-count convention – this differs from market to market, as shown in Figure 3.1. You should be aware of the day-count convention that applies to the bond you are buying before you buy it.

Calculating it – the Theory

Figure 3.2 shows the different numbers to be pulled from the sources described and how to use them to calculate the ratio.

Figure 3.2 Calculating the "Magic Number" for ... Accrued Interest

You have invested $10,000 in a Selenian government bond, the basic data on which is shown below:

Coupon 5%
Maturity date .... 30th November, 2010
Coupon dates .... 31st May and 30th November
Trade date .... 31st March, 2005
"Clean" price 98.73
Nominal amount purchased .... $10,129 ($10,000 × 100/98.73)
Day-count convention .... Actual/Actual
Ex-dividend period .... None
Settlement period .... Trade date + 3

Accrued interest is calculated by first working out the number of days between the settlement date and the last coupon date as follows:

Days accrued .... 123 days
(working)   [Settlement day (3rd April; Trade date + 3 days, is day 92) + days from 30th November to 31st December (31)]

Accrued interest (on price-only basis) is 1.685
(working)   (5 × 123/365)

The "dirty" price ("clean" + accrued interest) is 100.415
(working)   (98.73 + 1.685)

Accrued interest (money basis) is $170.67
(working)   (0.05 × (123/365) × 10129

ACCRUED INTEREST

CALCULATING IT FOR
JAPANESE GOVERNMENT BOND

Figure 3.3 Calculating Accrued Interest for the 10-year Japanese Government Bond

The figures ...

You have invested ¥100,000 in the JGB 1.3% 2014, which has the following characteristics ...

Coupon	1.30%
Last interest payment date	20th March, 2005
Maturity date	20th March, 2014
Maturity value	100
Date your purchase settles	15th April, 2005
Your purchase price is	98.31
Nominal amount purchased	¥101,719 (100,000 × 100/98.31)
Day-count convention	Actual/365
Ex-dividend period	None

The calculations ...

Days accrued .... 26 days
(working) [Settlement is day 105 minus coupon last paid on day 79]

Accrued interest (on price only basis) is 0.0926
(working) (1.3 × 26/365)

The "dirty" price ("clean" + accrued interest) is 98.4026
(working) (98.31 + 0.0926)

Accrued interest (money basis) is ¥94.19
(working) (0.013 × (26/365) × 101,719)

WHAT IT MEANS

Accrued interest is all about fairness. It is designed to give a fair apportionment of the interest that is clocking up on a bond so that the seller receives the interest earned from the last interest payment date up to the point the bond changes hands, and the buyer receives interest from that date onwards.

The new owner of the stock will receive the next interest payment in full, as if they had held the stock for the whole of the interest period. So when the deal is struck, as part of the price, the buyer pays the seller a small extra amount. That amount corresponds to the portion of the forthcoming interest payment that was "earned" by the seller before the stock changed hands.

This is the underlying principle to understand, and the details are simply extra little elaborations on top.

Remember, however, that the bond prices quoted in newspapers and financial websites are always "clean" prices – that is, they exclude accrued interest.

Where ex-dividend periods exist, in certain circumstances these can complicate the calculation of accrued interest. In some markets, bonds go "ex-dividend" a few days before a coupon payment. In the case of the UK government bond market, for example, this period is seven days.

An investor buying a bond during this period, even though it is before the coupon date, will not receive the coupon. Interest will only begin accruing from the coupon payment date a few days later. In circumstances like this, when stocks change hands during an ex-dividend period, accrued interest is negative, and the "dirty" price paid by the buyer is actually less than the "clean" price.

It is relatively rare for an ex-dividend period to affect an accrued interest calculation, and financial calculators rarely take this factor into account. However, if you are buying a bond just prior to a coupon payment date in a market that operates an ex-dividend period, it makes sense to check this situation.

Accrued interest and whether or not a bond has a high or low coupon matter because they can have tax implications. Low-coupon bonds generate more of their return in the form of capital gains. High-coupon bonds generate more of their return in the form of interest paid and accrued.

Whether you should prefer one to the other depends on the relative rates of tax on income and capital gains you are likely to bear. Some government bonds are exempt from capital gains tax and, if you have no requirement for income, it makes sense to buy a low-coupon bond in these circumstances.

MAGIC NUMBER 4

Running Yield

THE DEFINITION

Running yield, sometimes called "current yield" or "simple yield", is the basic expression of the relationship between a bond's fixed interest rate, or coupon, and its price. The coupon is expressed as a percentage of the market price, with any accrued interest being ignored.

A halfway house between the running yield and the redemption yield (covered in Magic Number 5) is the adjusted current yield (ACY). This takes account of the difference between the current price of the bond and its redemption value, according to the formula given below. The ACY is widely used in the Japanese bond market and is sometimes called the "Japanese Simple Yield".

THE FORMULAS

$$RY = (coupon/\text{"clean" price}) \times 100$$

$$ACY = RY + (100 - \text{"clean" price})/\text{Years to Maturity}$$

In other words, the ACY adjusts the running yield by adding (or, if negative subtracting) the annualized change between the current price and the redemption price.

THE COMPONENTS

Coupon – this is the stated interest rate on the bond. Bonds are usually described in terms such as "5% Treasury stock 2014". The coupon on the bond in this case is 5%.

"Clean" price – the current price of the bond. Par value is normally 100% and bonds are usually priced in percentages relative to this figure. A bond standing below par might be priced at, say, 95 (or 95% – the percent sign is usually omitted). The "clean" price excludes accrued interest.

Maturity date and par value – if a bond matures in four years' time, currently stands at 95 and has a par (or redemption) value of 100, it might be assumed to appreciate at 1.29% a year between now and its maturity date. This is the basis for adjusting the running yield to calculate the ACY.

Where's the Data?

Coupon, maturity date and "clean" price – bond details in newspapers and financial websites usually state these three elements. But the precise month and day of redemption should be checked.

The reason for the need for precision with respect to dates and price is that these will be important in getting an accurate adjustment to the yield in the case of the ACY.

Par value – this is the price at which the bond will be redeemed, and is assumed to be 100, unless otherwise stated.

Period to maturity – to get to this number, used in the calculation of the ACY, the current date is subtracted from the redemption date and the result expressed in years and fractions of a year in decimals.

Hence, the UK Treasury 5% stock 2014 has a coupon of 5%, is repaid at par and, according to data from the *Financial Times*, for example, pays interest on 7th March and 7th September. Its redemption date is 7th September, 2014. If you bought the stock on 7th April, 2005, this means the period to maturity would be nine years and five months which, expressed in decimals, is 9.4166 years.

CALCULATING IT – THE THEORY

Figure 4.1 shows the different numbers to be pulled from the sources described and how to use them to calculate the ratio.

Figure 4.1 Calculating the "Magic Number" for ... Running Yield and Adjusted Current Yield

The Martian government has issued a bond, the basic data on which is shown below:

Coupon 5%
Maturity date .... 30th November, 2010
Today's date .... 31st March, 2005
"Clean" price 98.73
Redemption value 100
Period to maturity is .... 5 years 8 months (or 5.66 years)

Running yield is 5.06%
(working) .... (5/98.73) × 100

Adjusted current yield is 5.28%
(working) .... 5.06 + (100 − 98.73)/5.66

This is the movement between the current price and redemption price averaged over 5.66 years added to the previously calculated running yield.

CALCULATING IT FOR
UK TREASURY

Figure 4.2 Calculating Running Yield and Adjusted Current Yield for the UK Treasury 8% 2015

The figures ...

Coupon 8%
Maturity date .... 7th December, 2015
Today's date .... 31st March, 2005
"Clean" price 127.65
Redemption value 100
Period to maturity is .... 10 years 252 days (or 10.69 years)

The calculations ...

Running yield is 6.27%
(working)   (8/127.65) × 100

Adjusted current yield is 3.68%
(working)   6.27 + (100 − 127.65)/10.69
                                                          or 6.27 + (−2.59)
                                                          or 6.27 − 2.59

This shows that the adjustment can be negative if a bond currently stands substantially above its redemption value.

WHAT IT MEANS

The advantage of the running yield is that it is simple to calculate and shows the most important attribute of bonds. This is the inverse relationship between a bond's yield and its price.

It is easy to grasp if you imagine a bond with a coupon of 5% and a price of 100. The running yield is 5%. If the price were 50, the yield would be 10% (5 × 100/50). This is because the £5 of income on a bond with a face value of £100 could be bought for half-price. If the bond's price were 200, the yield would be 2.5% (5 × 100/200). This is because the bond's £5 of income would cost double the bond's face value and therefore the return would be cut accordingly.

This is a very important concept to understand because, other things being equal, bond prices respond to the general level of interest rates.

If rates are rising or seen as likely to go up in the near future, then bond prices will fall. Falling rates produce rising bond prices.

The two different examples given earlier are not typical of what really happens in the bond market on a day-to-day basis. Many bonds stay fairly close to their par value for much of their life. In this instance, the running yield and the adjusted current yield give results that can help investors work out the true returns from the bonds without too much fuss or complexity.

In the case of the example shown in Figure 4.1, the actual redemption yield on the bond (see Magic Number 5 to learn how to calculate it) is 5.26%, so that the adjusted current yield is a close enough approximation for most people.

This is not true in the case of bonds with high coupons. If the prevailing level of interest rates is some way below the coupon level, then bonds like this will inevitably stand well above their par value. Investors buying them on this basis need to balance the extra income earned in the short term, as expressed by the running yield, with the decrease in capital value that will occur during the period before the bonds are repaid at their par value. In the example given in Figure 4.2, for instance, the running yield of 6.27% is much higher than the prevailing level of interest rates (around 4%–4.5% at the time of writing).

The ACY presents one way of adjusting for this, by subtracting the average annual decrease in value that can be expected between now and the bond's maturity date.

In cases like this, however, the ACY can be misleading. For one thing, the decrease in value may not occur uniformly over the 10-year period. Secondly this calculation ignores the fact that high levels of interest are being received from the bond in the meantime, which can in turn be reinvested to earn further interest. This interest-on-interest component is not reflected in the bond's adjusted current yield, which is actually significantly lower than the true return on the bond, as expressed by the redemption yield. The redemption yield (see Magic Number 5) is actually 4.68%, a full percentage point higher than the ACY.

In other words, the running yield is a good guide to the return we'll get on our money invested in the bond in the short term. The ACY can be used in some instances, but in others it may be misleading.

With this in mind, in the next section we'll go on to look at the most accurate way of expressing a bond's true return. This is the redemption yield or yield to maturity.

Redemption Yield

The Definition

The redemption yield is sometimes called "yield to maturity" (YTM).

In simple terms, the redemption yield has three components: the "running yield" (see Magic Number 4); interest-on-interest that would be earned if successive interest payments were reinvested (see the compounding concept explained in Magic Number 1); and the annual rate of capital gain or loss that would be made if a bond were held until maturity and repaid at its par (or nominal) value, which is usually 100% of face value.

In strict terms, the redemption yield is the uniform discount rate at which the present value of a bond's future cash flows (that is, its coupon payments, interest on coupon payments, and repayment of the bond's face value) equates to its current price, including accrued interest. We covered the concept of discounting and present value in Magic Number 2 and accrued interest in Magic Number 3.

The Formula

YTM = running yield + "interest-on-interest" + annualized gain or loss on maturity.

Alternatively, it can be found as follows:

PV of bond cash flows discounted at r% = market price + accrued interest

Where r% = redemption yield.

The Components

Coupon – this is the stated interest rate on the bond. Bonds are usually described in terms such as "5% Treasury Stock 2014". The coupon on the bond in this case is 5%.

Net price – the current price of the bond. Par value is normally 100% and bonds are usually priced in percentages relative to this figure. A bond standing below par might be priced at, say, 95 (or 95% – the percent sign is usually omitted).

Accrued interest – market prices are stated net of any interest that has accrued since the last interest date, but this is added to/subtracted from dealing prices for buyers/sellers as appropriate. This concept is explained in detail in Magic Number 3. There are several conventions for calculating it.

Maturity date and par value – if a bond matures in four years' time, currently stands at 95 and has a par value (or value at redemption) of 100, it might be assumed to appreciate at 1.29% a year between now and its maturity date.

Where's the Data?

Coupon, maturity, and net price – bond details in newspapers and financial websites usually state all three elements. But the precise month and day of redemption should be checked, as should the frequency of interest payments.

Accrued interest – this is calculated automatically in some financial calculators or can be worked out, as described in Magic Number 3, by subtracting the deal date from the last interest date to get the number of days over which interest has accrued and then pro-rating accordingly.

Calculating it – the Theory

Figure 5.1 shows how the redemption yield can be calculated in a fictional example. Because the calculation is complex, redemption yields are calculated in one of several ways. Specialized books of tables can be used, reading across from the appropriate maturity and coupon for a given price. There are online redemption-yield calculators. And desktop financial calculators now have the facility to calculate redemption yields, the process being described briefly in Figure 5.2.

Figure 5.1 Calculating the "Magic Number" for ... Redemption Yield

A Venusian government bond has:

A coupon paid twice yearly of 3.75%
The deal settles on .... 15th April, 2005
The bond is redeemed at 100 on .... 3rd September, 2009
Its price is .... 96.84 + accrued interest of 0.44

Using a Texas Instruments BAII Plus financial calculator **the redemption yield (or yield to maturity) is**... **4.55%**

In other words, the current running yield is supplemented by the gain in price from 97.28 (net price plus accrued interest) to 100 over a period of approxiately four years and five months.

CALCULATING IT FOR
US TREASURY

Figure 5.2 shows how the numbers related to this US government stock combine to produce the "magic number", with the calculation performed using a financial calculator.

Figure 5.2 Calculating the Redemption Yield for the 4% US Treasury Note 2014

The figures ...

Interest payment frequency .... 2 times per year
Interest payment dates ....15th February and 15th August
Maturity date ....15th February, 2014
Maturity value 100
Date your purchase settles .... 15th April, 2005
Your purchase price is... 98.62

The calculation ...

Key these variables into the Texas Instruments BAII financial calculator after pressing 2nd (second function) BOND to access the worksheet.

Accrued interest is calculated automatically at.. 0.65

Tab down to YLD (for redemption yield) and press CPT (to compute)

The redemption yield (or YTM) is 4.19%

The value can be checked against the redemption yield quoted in the financial press for that particular day.

The screenshot on the opposite page shows the same calculation performed using an online bond calculator (at www.calculatorweb.com). This shows the yield at 4.12%, which is clearly less accurate, possibly because it may not take into account the incidence of accrued interest or assume semi-annual interest payments.

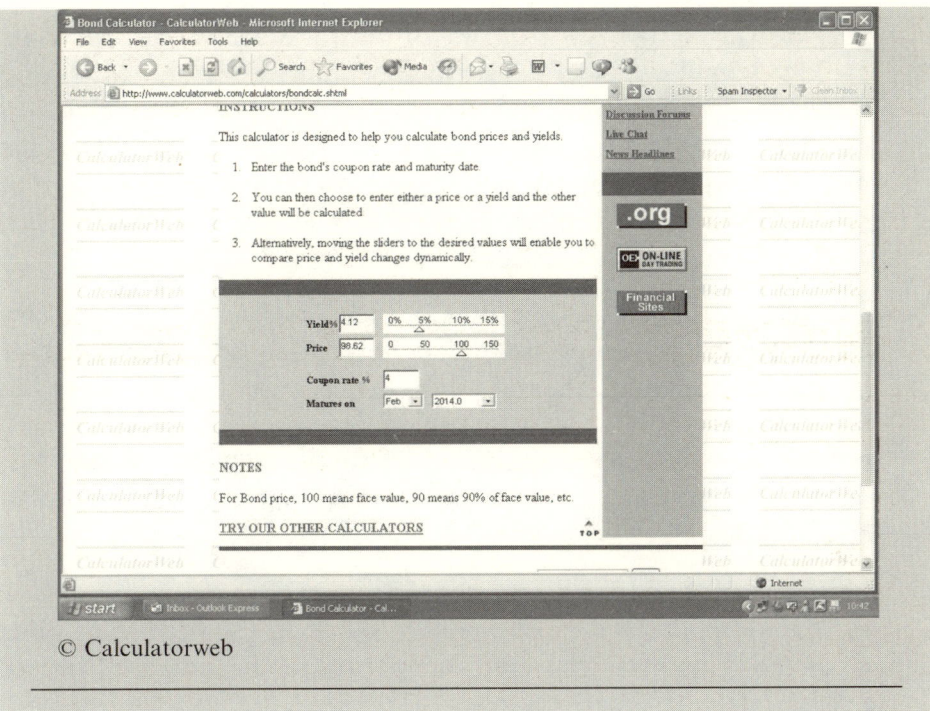

© Calculatorweb

In practice, bond redemption yields (always counted gross – that is, before any tax on dividends or capital gain) can be found from a financial newspaper or website, but it is important to be aware of the nature of the components that go to make up the yield. Because in some markets income and capital may be taxed at different rates, even if two bonds have the same gross redemption yield, one bond may be preferred over another for tax reasons.

What it Means

Bond yields are the basis for many other financial calculations. Redemption yields on government bonds have at least three major uses:

- as an indicator of economic health. Bonds with less time to run to maturity normally stand on lower yields than those that have redemption dates further in the future. This is because investors would rather have money now or within a short time in the future than wait longer for it. This relationship between yields of bonds of lengthening redemption dates is called the "yield curve". (This is examined in detail in Magic Number 10.)

- as a measure of the risk-free rate of return. Since G7 governments are highly unlikely to default on their debt, invest in their bonds and there is virtually guaranteed repayment of capital – at par value – on maturity. The yield to maturity is therefore an indicator of what the market views as the annual risk-free rate of return for that period of time. This concept is often used to establish a rate at which to discount future profits, dividends and cash flow.

- as a measure of credit quality. US Treasury Bonds and Treasury Notes are, by convention, the benchmark against which all other bonds are measured. The difference between yields of bonds of the same maturity is known as the "spread" (or, occasionally, "basis") and is usually measured in basis points where one basis point (bp) represents one-hundredth of one percent. Spreads and how to calculate them are covered in Magic Number 9.

All this talk of "risk-free rates" should not lead investors to imagine that bonds like this are intrinsically risk-free in terms of their price movements. The term "risk-free" simply means in this case "free of the risk of default".

You are never guaranteed to make money in a bond. Bond prices move up and down in inverse relationship to interest rates, since the latter influence yield expectations and, hence, bond prices.

Equally, because the return of a bond held to maturity is fixed and predictable, inflation is the big enemy of bonds.

Conventional bonds do best when prospects for company profits, and hence the outlook for equities, are worsening, and when there is deflationary pressure rather than inflation. In circumstances like this, bank interest rates will be very low indeed, with bonds much the best home for money.

At other times, when inflation is rising and interest rates are likely to move up sharply to counter it, bonds may prove very poor investments, and their prices may fall substantially.

MAG1C NUM8ER 6

Yield on a Zero-coupon Bond

THE DEFINITION

A zero-coupon bond, as its name suggests, is a bond that pays no income. Bonds like this are issued at a big discount to their redemption value, and all of their return comes in the form of capital growth. The yield to maturity is, in effect, the annualized compound rate of capital growth from the price you pay to the price at which the bond is redeemed.

THE FORMULA

To get the yield to maturity on a zero-coupon bond, we can adapt the formula we used in Magic Number 1 when calculating compound interest. That formula was:

$FV = P \times (1 + R)^n$

In the case of the zero-coupon bond, the formula becomes:

Par Value = Current price $\times (1 + R)^n$

In this formula, R is the annual yield to maturity, and n is the number of years to maturity.

We can rearrange this to get the formula for R, if necessary. But, in reality, calculating the yield on a zero-coupon bond can be done easily using the "compound rate of growth" function in a financial calculator.

The Components

Par value – this is the price at which the bond is redeemed at maturity. As described earlier, in most cases, par value is 100% of nominal value – that is, the full face value of the bond.

Price paid – this is self-explanatory. All bond prices are usually quoted as a percentage of nominal or par value. Zero-coupon bonds are issued and normally trade at a significant discount to par value.

Time to maturity – the terms of the bond specify the maturity date, when the bond is repaid at par. Work out the remaining life of the bond in years, or years and parts of a year expressed as a decimal. This is then plugged into the formula.

Where's the Data?

Par value – the price at which the bond is redeemed will be stated in the prospectus when the bond is issued.

Redemption date – the redemption date will be stated in the prospectus when the bond is issued, and in financial newspapers and on financial websites. Having said that, information on zero-coupon bonds is not that easy to come by. You may have to rely on your broker to provide you with the necessary information.

Current price – as with the above, prices for zero-coupon bonds can be hard to find in the press. They are available from some newspapers, some financial websites or, more likely, from brokers.

Calculating it – the Theory

Figure 6.1 shows the different numbers to be pulled from the sources described on p. 38 and how to use them to calculate the ratio using a financial calculator.

> **Figure 6.1   Calculating the "Magic Number" for ... Yield on a Zero-coupon Bond**
>
> Martian Widget Industries has issued a Eurodollar zero-coupon bond. Its terms are:
>
> Amount .... $500 m
> Maturity .... December 31st, 2012
> Coupon 0%
> Issue price 60.0%
> Redemption price 100.0%
> Current price 62.4%
> Today's date .... March 5th, 2005
>
> Calculate the unexpired life of the bond. This is six years plus the difference between 5th March (day 64) and 31st December (day 365).
>
> Unexpired life is 6.825
> (working)   6 + (365 − 64)/365
>
> Using the annualized percentage change feature on a financial calculator, input the following in this order:
>
> | | | | |
> |---|---|---|---|
> | Old | input | 62.4 | ENTER |
> | New | input | 100 | ENTER |
> | Period | input | 6.825 | ENTER |
> | % change | COMPUTE ... | | |
>
> ... gives the answer ...   7.15%
> This is the yield on the bond.

CALCULATING IT FOR
SEK HK

Figure 6.2   Calculating the Zero-coupon Yield on the SEK HK$ Zero-coupon Bond Due 2018

The figures ...

The terms of the bond, which was issued in April 2004, are:

Amount .... HK$ 204 m
Maturity .... 28th December, 2018
Coupon 0%
Redemption 100%

The deal settles on 1st March, 2005. The bond, which is unlisted, is currently changing hands at 53%.

The calculations ...

Step 1: Calculate the unexpired term of the bond.

This is 13 years plus the number of days from 1st March (day 60) to 28th December (day 362).

Unexpired term is   13.827
(working) .... (13 + (362 − 60)/365

Step 2: Using the annualized percentage change feature on a financial calculator, input the following in this order:

Old	input	53 ENTER
New	input	100 ENTER
Period	input	13.827 ENTER
% change	COMPUTE ...	

... gives the answer...   **4.70%**

This is the yield on the bond.

WHAT IT MEANS

You might think that a bond with no coupon is the very opposite of what bond investing is really about. However, bonds like this have some advantages. One of the big ones is that they benefit those whose income may be taxed at a high rate but who have lower, or no, tax to pay on capital gains.

They also avoid two of the problems that beset coupon-bearing bonds. The first is, that to take full advantage of compounding, you have to assume that you will have the discipline not to spend the investment income you receive. Secondly, even if you do have that discipline, you must be able to reinvest the interest you receive at the same rate of return as you receive on the bond. Zero-coupon bonds take this task away from you. There is no coupon to reinvest. What you see is what you get.

While many zero-coupon bonds originate from corporate issuers, such as the SEK issue used in Figure 6.2, they are also a feature of many government bond markets. A conventional government bond can be broken down into a series (or strip) of zero-coupon bonds.

The way strips work is roughly as follows.

A conventional bond is bought in the market by a market-maker or investment bank.

The number of coupons remaining to maturity and their value are calculated and stripped into the same number of separate securities each with a nominal value equating to the coupon. Each of these becomes a separate zero-coupon bond.

The principal repayment becomes a further zero-coupon stock, with a much higher nominal value.

This is shown in the example in Figure 6.3.

Figure 6.3 Creating a "Strip" of Zero-coupon Bonds

The UK Treasury 5.75% 2009 pays interest semi-annually and matures on 7th December, 2009.

It is now 1st January, 2005. A bank purchases £100,000 nominal of the stocks. It creates the following strip of 11 zero-coupon bonds.

Bond	Maturity date (7th of ...)	Maturity value (£)	Origin
Zero 1	Jun-05	5,750	Coupon
Zero 2	Dec-05	5,750	Coupon
Zero 3	Jun-06	5,750	Coupon
Zero 4	Dec-06	5,750	Coupon
Zero 5	Jun-07	5,750	Coupon
Zero 6	Dec-07	5,750	Coupon
Zero 7	Jun-08	5,750	Coupon
Zero 8	Dec-08	5,750	Coupon
Zero 9	Jun-09	5,750	Coupon
Zero 10	Dec-09	5,750	Coupon
Zero 11	Dec-09	100,000	Principal

All of these securities trade separately and will have different prices.

Most investors in zero-coupon bonds are pension funds, but zeros also appeal to others. These are frugal standard-rate taxpayers with low current income requirements but sizeable capital. There is an obvious section of the population that falls into this category: doting grandparents who want to provide for their grandchildren's education. In other words, zero-coupon bonds appeal to those with a specific savings target several years hence.

We need to sound a word of warning about investing in zeros. Their prices are inherently more volatile than other bonds. This is because their price is highly sensitive to the expected levels of interest rates, which in turn affect the discount rate the market assumes in order to arrive at the appropriate price. The longer the time to maturity, the more sensitive the price will be to changes in the assumed rate of interest/discount rate.

It is easy to illustrate this phenomenon. Assume that two zero-coupon bonds from the same issuer have maturity dates respectively five and 15 years in the future. Assuming both are on a 5% yield basis, the price of the five-year bond would be 78.35, and the price of the 15-year bond would be 48.10. If they now both moved onto a 6% yield basis, the price of both bonds would fall. The price of the five-year bond would fall to 74.73 (a drop of 4.6%) and the price of the 15-year bond to 41.73 (a drop of 13.2%).

These calculations can be performed easily in the "compound growth rate" function on a financial calculator by entering the par ("new") value, period and percentage change figures as inputs, and then computing the original "old" price.

Yield to Worst

The Definition

Yield to worst (or "worst-case yield") is another variant of the redemption yield. It is one that is tailored to coping with bonds that have a specific feature. This feature allows the issuer to redeem the bond early at a specific time or price, or after a specific date at a preset price. These are known as "callable" bonds. The yield to worst (YTW), simply consists of substituting the call prices and dates for the full-term redemption value and normal maturity date and finding the combination of terms that gives the worst (i.e. lowest) yield.

Bonds like this always have a call schedule that is determined at the time of issue. This sets out the terms under which the bond can be "called"; that is, the option to redeem can be exercised by the issuer. If bonds are redeemed early, it will often be at a slight premium to the par value. If a bond has a particularly generous call provision, it may be that it is in the investor's interest for the bond to be called early. In this case, the yield to worst will be the current redemption yield.

The Formula

YTW = lowest of RY; RYC1; RYC2 etc.

Where:

RY = yield to normal maturity

RYC1 = yield based on price and term at first call period

RYC2 = yield based on price and term at second call period

The Components

Price – this is the market price of the bond.

Coupon and maturity – these are basic terms of the bond. We need to know the frequency of coupon payments – whether, for example, the coupon is paid annually or in two semi-annual installments – and the precise date of the maturity.

Call feature – the call feature is a specific part of the bond's terms at the time of issue. It will take the form of a schedule showing the dates and prices at which the bond can be "called"; that is, redeemed at the issuer's option.

Redemption yields – the procedure is to calculate the redemption yield based on the current price assuming redemption at par on the normal maturity date, and the redemption yields based on the assumptions that the price and date of each specific option for calling the bond are the redemption price and maturity.

Call option type – call features that specify the call being exercised on specific days are known as "European calls". Those that specify the call being exercised from a specific date onwards are known as "American calls". This has nothing whatever to do with the origin of the bond's issuer or the currency in which it is denominated, but is simply a convention used in the market. In the case of an American call, the yield to worst will most probably be the yield at the point the call option becomes exercisable.

Where's the Data?

Coupon and maturity – bond details in newspapers and financial websites usually state these elements. But the precise month and day of redemption should be checked, as should the frequency of interest payments.

Call feature – this should be available from the bond's original prospectus, from a broker, direct from the issuer's website or from a bond-orientated statistical service.

Net price – this is the market price of the bond and should be available from a financial newspaper or a bond-related website.

Calculating it – the Theory

Figure 7.1 shows the different numbers to be pulled from the sources described and how to use them to calculate the ratio.

Figure 7.1 Calculating the "Magic Numbers" for … Yield to Worst

Solar System Enterprises has issued a bond with the following terms and call feature:

Coupon 6%
Coupon frequency .... Semi-annual
Maturity date .... 10th August, 2009
Callable at: .... 101 on 10th August, 2007
                                                                                    100 on 10th August, 2008
Current price 102
Settlement date .... 31st March, 2005

Using a Texas Instruments BAII Plus financial calculator, we can compute the yields as follows:

| Yield to maturity is: | A. | 5.48% |
| Yield to first call is: | B. | 5.48% |

This is the YTM calculated using 101 as redemption price and 10th August, 2007 as redemption date.

| Yield to second call is: | C. | 5.34% |

This is the YTM calculated using 100 as redemption price and 10th August, 2008 as redemption date.

Yield to worst is: **5.34%**
(working)   (lowest of A, B, or C)

YIELD TO WORST

CALCULATING IT FOR
LOWER COLORADO RIVER AUTHORITY

Figure 7.2   Calculating Yield to Worst for Lower Colorado River Authority 5.875% 2016

The figures ...

The Lower Colorado River Authority has issued a bond with the following terms and call feature:

Coupon 5.875%
Coupon frequency .... Semi-annual
Maturity date .... 15th May, 2016
Callable at: .... 101 on 15th May, 2009
                                                                                  100 on 15th May, 2010
Current price 110.759
Today's date .... 23rd April, 2004

Using a Texas Instruments BAII Plus financial calculator, we can compute the yields as follows:

Yield to maturity is: A.   4.70%
Yield to first call is: B.   3.70%

This is the YTM calculated using 101 as redemption price and 15th May, 2009 as redemption date.

Yield to second call is: C.   3.87%

This is the YTM calculated using 100 as redemption price and 15th May, 2010 as redemption date.

Yield to worst is: 3.70%
(working)   (lowest of A, B, or C)

WHAT IT MEANS

Once you become accustomed to calculating redemption yields, working out the yield to worst on a bond with a call feature is no big deal. And there is one important reason for looking at this particular number.

It is that this is a calculation that the issuer, who has the option to call the bond, can do equally well. The worst yield result from the point of view of the holder of the bond will be the best yield result for the issuer of the bond. It is therefore the point at which the option to redeem is most likely to be exercised, other things being equal.

The call feature gives the issuer of the bond a play on interest rates. If funding costs have dropped in the time between the bond's issue and the time the first call kicks in, it will be worthwhile for the issuer to redeem the bond and issue a new one at a lower yield.

If interest rates have stayed the same in the meantime, the issuer simply lets the initial call option lapse and allows the bond to run to the next (if there are two) or to maturity.

The same process can be done with "puttable" bonds. Puttable bonds give the holder of the bond (rather than the issuer) the option to redeem the bond early, normally on specific dates and perhaps at a slight discount to the full redemption value; effectively the mirror image of the situation with the callable bond. Once again we can calculate the yields implied by normal redemption and by redemption based on the terms indicated by the put feature.

In this case, the yield to worst is the highest of the yields, the most attractive strategy for the holder, and the worst-case scenario for the issuer.

Callable bonds are common in some markets, such as the US municipal (muni) bond market, and generally bonds with features like this are also quite common in the Eurobond arena.

A range of additional terms is also used in this area. Many are self-explanatory, such as "yield to next call" and "yield to refunding". Yield to refunding occurs when a bond is currently callable but the terms of the bond are such that some additional conditions have to be satisfied before the bond can be redeemed. Typically this is to prevent an issuer issuing a new bond and calling and redeeming an existing bond using the proceeds. The refunding date, which will be in the original bond prospectus, is the earliest date the bonds can be redeemed using the proceeds of a lower-cost bond issue.

One interesting point about callable and puttable bonds is that in effect they combine a conventional bond and an option. In the case of the callable bond, a purchaser is buying a "straight" bond and at the same time granting (or "writing", as the jargon has it) a call option over it to the issuer. In the case of a puttable bond, the buyer of the bond is getting a straight bond and a put option (written by the issuer) bound together in the price he pays at the outset for the bond.

As we will find out in Part Three of this book, it is perfectly possible to value these two component parts separately. Some traders have made a good living over the years by valuing callable and puttable bonds in this way and by exploiting the anomalies in pricing that may be uncovered as a result.

Redemption Yield on an Index-linked Bond

THE DEFINITIONS

Index-linked bonds adjust principal amount invested, and therefore the coupon payments related to it, to a measure of inflation such as the retail price index (RPI) in the UK, or the CPI in the USA.

This means that future coupon payments and the eventual repayment amount of the bond cannot be fixed with precision. Because of this, calculating returns on bonds like this involves making assumptions about likely future inflation rates. Working out the redemption yield in these circumstances involves using an internal rate of return (IRR) calculation.

The IRR is a percentage used to express the return required to equate the cost of an investment, especially one that generates irregular amounts of income (and in some cases periodic intermediate costs), with the proceeds received when it is sold or redeemed. IRRs were covered in depth in Magic Number 29 of the original *Magic Numbers* book.

In its simplest form, where a single purchase and a single sale are made, and no income is received in the meantime, the IRR is the compound annual rate of return calculated from the purchase price to the sale price. So the return on a zero-coupon bond, as shown earlier in Magic Number 6, is in effect an IRR calculation.

In the case of more complex calculations, involving either irregularly timed investments, variable amounts of periodic income, and variable sale or redemption proceeds (or any combination of these), you can usually do the calculation fairly easily using a spreadsheet.

In the case of an index-linked bond, the information required is the amount of the original investment made (this is the bond's "dirty" price, recorded in the spreadsheet as a negative); a series of amounts of income received during the life of the investment; and the amount of the redemption proceeds (usually par value of 100 plus the final coupon, both adjusted for the indexation factor).

IRRs can be calculated using a financial calculator or a pre-set "function" in a spreadsheet program such as Microsoft Excel. An assumption needs to be made of the likely rate of inflation over the life of the bond. The coupons and repayment are then adjusted to reflect this and the separate items put in a schedule as positive amounts. The amount invested is put at the head of the column as a negative amount, and the IRR is calculated in the normal way.

The real yield is then calculated by stripping out the assumed inflation factor from the calculation using a simple formula.

The implied rate of inflation expected by the market (the so-called break-even rate of inflation or BEI) is normally calculated as an approximation by subtracting the index-linked yield from the yield on a conventional government bond of the same maturity.

The Formulas

Nominal yield

The formula for this calculation is extremely complex but basically takes the form:

$$Y = \text{IRR for } (C1 \times I)...(C2 \times I)...(C3 \times I)... \text{ etc. } ...((Cn + P) \times I) \text{ and } -DP$$

Where:

Y = nominal redemption yield on index-linked bond

$C1$ etc. = coupon series

I = inflation adjustment (different in each case, based on inflation rate and RPI)

P = principal repayment

DP = "dirty" price (market price plus accrued interest)

Real redemption yield

For a bond that pays coupons once a year, this is found according to the formula

$$1 + RY = (1 + ny)/(1 + i)$$

For a bond that pays coupons twice yearly, the formula is

$$(1 + 0.5RY)^2 = (1 + 0.5ny)^2 / (1 + i)$$

Taking the square root of the resulting number and subtracting 1 then produces RY.

All yield amounts in the formulas are expressed in decimals.

In both cases,

RY = real yield

ny = nominal yield

i = assumed inflation rate

Approximate break-even rate of inflation

BEI = RY of non-index-linked bond − RY of index-linked bond of same maturity

THE COMPONENTS

Dirty price – this is the market price of the bond plus accrued interest. Accrued interest is calculated according to the method explained in Magic Number 3.

Coupon – this is the nominal coupon on the bond. As demonstrated above, the IRR calculation method can work equally well for bonds that pay interest once yearly or twice yearly.

Principal – this is the nominal, face or par value of the bond, as described in previous sections.

Assumed inflation rate – this is the rate of inflation assumed to hold good for the purposes of projecting forward the RPI numbers to

REDEMPTION YIELD ON AN INDEX-LINKED BOND

make the necessary adjustments to coupon payments and principal repayments.

RPI adjustment basis – adjustments to coupon amounts and principal repayment are made on the basis of dividing the appropriate RPI number for a particular coupon payment (and/or principal repayment) by the appropriate RPI number for the date the bond was issued. RPI numbers are normally lagged.

In the case of the UK, for example, index-linked bonds operate on the basis of RPI figures eight months prior. For example, the adjustment factor for a coupon payable in December would be found by dividing the previous April's RPI number by the RPI number eight months prior to the payment date in question.

WHERE'S THE DATA?

Dirty Price – the net price of the bond can be found from a financial newspaper or website. Accrued interest can be estimated in the usual way using a financial calculator and calculating the unexpired time to the next coupon payment.

Coupon – this is the nominal coupon on the bond and will be explicitly stated in the terms of the bond, and usually also in the usual places in financial newspapers and websites.

Principal – repayment at maturity is generally at par plus the inflation adjustment based on the appropriate lagged RPI figure at the date of issue. Note that, as with a normal bond, this does not mean that an investor who buys above par will have his investment fully indexed, but only the nominal value of the bonds acquired at that time, based on the adjustment factor from time of issue. The example on page 55 makes it clear how this works.

Assumed inflation rate – in most markets there is a convention about the assumed rate of inflation used to project forward RPI numbers. In the UK, for example, a figure of 3% is used. In some instances, yields are calculated on two different inflation bases.

RPI adjustment basis – RPI numbers (or, for example, the CPI-U number in the US) can usually be found from the national statistics organization of the country and the time lag assumed from the terms of the bonds as stated at the issuer's website or in the bond's prospectus.

CALCULATING IT – THE THEORY

Figure 8.1 shows the different numbers from the sources described and how to use them to calculate the ratio.

Figure 8.1 Calculating the "Magic Number" for ... Nominal and Real Yield on an Index-linked Bond

The government of Uranus has just issued an index-linked bond. Its terms are as follows:

Coupon .... 5% × indexation adjustment
Interest payment date .... 31st December
Redemption date .... 31st December, 2010
Redemption value.. 100 × indexation adjustment
Calculation basis for indexing .... RPI nine months prior
RPI at date of issue minus nine months 106
RPI now 110
Expected inflation rate .... 3% pa
Current price of the bond... 120

It is now 31st March, 2005. Work out the redemption yield assuming 3% inflation.

	Base amount		RPI	RPI Adjustment	Adjusted amount
					−120.00
Dec-05	5	C	110.0	1.038	5.19
(Working)				(110/106)	(5 × 1.038)
Dec-06	5	C	113.3	1.069	5.34
(Working)			(110 × 1.03)	(113.3/106)	(5 × 1.069)
Dec-07	5	C	116.7	1.101	5.50
(Working)			(110 × 1.03^2)	(116.7/106)	(5 × 1.101)
Dec-08	5	C	120.2	1.134	5.67
(Working)			(110 × 1.03^3)	(120.2/106)	(5 × 1.134)
Dec-09	5	C	123.8	1.168	5.84
(Working)			(110 × 1.03^4)	(123.8/106)	(5 × 1.168)
Dec-10	105	C + P	127.5	1.203	126.30
(Working)			(110 × 1.03^5)	(127.5/106)	(105 × 1.203)

Nominal redemption yield (calculated as IRR of these flows of cash)   4.68%

Real yield, from the formula at the start of the section, is: 0.0163   (or 1.68%)
(working) .... (1.0468/1.03) − 1

Note that the principal repayment is 127.5, only 6.25% above the price paid, even though there have been five years of inflation at 3% assumed.

REDEMPTION YIELD ON AN INDEX-LINKED BOND

CALCULATING IT FOR
US TREASURY TIPS

Figure 8.2 Calculating Yield and BEI for the 2% TIPS 2014

This example uses one of the Treasury Inflation Projected Securities (or TIPS) issued by the US Treasury, in this case the inflation-indexed 2% Treasury note.

The US Treasury issued this stock on 15th January, 2004. It is linked to the CPI-U index of US inflation. Other details on the bond are given below.

Coupon .... 2% x indexation adjustment
Interest payment dates .... 15th July and 15th January
Redemption date .... 15th January, 2014
Redemption value .... 100 × indexation adjustment
Calculation basis for indexing .... CPI-U three months prior
Reference CPI-U at date of issue 184.7742
CPI-U now 186.2
Expected inflation rate 2.50%
Current market price of the bond 101.25
Accrued interest (actual/actual) 0.59
(working)   1 × (108 days/183 days)

It is now 1st May, 2004. Work out the redemption yield assuming 2.5% inflation.

Base amount			CPI-U	Adjustment factor	Adjusted amount
					−101.84 (dirty price)
Jul-04	1	C	187.084	1.013	1.01
Jan-05	1	C	189.422	1.025	1.03
Jul-05	1	C	191.789	1.038	1.04
Jan-06	1	C	194.186	1.051	1.05
Jul-06	1	C	196.614	1.064	1.06
Jan-07	1	C	199.072	1.077	1.08
Jul-07	1	C	201.560	1.091	1.09
Jan-08	1	C	204.080	1.104	1.10
Jul-08	1	C	206.630	1.118	1.12
Jan-09	1	C	209.212	1.132	1.13
Jul-09	1	C	211.827	1.146	1.15
Jan-10	101	C+P	214.475	1.161	117.23

Redemption yield (calculated as IRR of these flows of cash)   **2.10%**

The redemption yield on the conventional 10-year Treasury note is currently 4.45%. By the quick method of calculation, the **breakeven rate of inflation** is **2.35%**.

This is the conventional yield (4.45%) minus the index-linked yield (2.1%).

What it Means

The real yield on inflation-linked bonds is the main parameter used to evaluate them. This is because it strips out any assumptions that we might make about the likely rate of inflation. Once this is done, we can evaluate the bonds much as we would do conventional ones, and as discussed earlier in Magic Number 5.

However, there is another number that is much simpler to calculate that gives us some useful information about the economy and the market in general. This is the breakeven rate of inflation (BEI). This is the rate of inflation above which it would be better to hold an inflation-linked bond than a conventional one with the same maturity. Alternatively, it is the rate of inflation being predicted for the immediate future.

As explained earlier, the formula normally used to calculate the BEI is simply the yield on a conventional government bond minus the yield on the inflation-linked equivalent of the same maturity.

Devotees of the intricacies of compounding will notice that this way of calculating the BEI, while generally accepted in the market, is not strictly correct. In fact, the correct way of calculating for a bond that pays coupons twice yearly is by dividing the square of 1 plus half the nominal bond yield by the square of 1 plus half the yield on the index-linked bond, and then subtracting 1 from the result.

The reason that the approximation is used is that there are plenty of sources of error in the calculation as it is, not least because the match between the redemption dates of the two bonds being compared may not be exactly the same, and also because of the lag used in calculating the inflation adjustment.

The BEI calculated in this way generally has a fairly good, though imperfect, record in predicting inflation about six months ahead. The imperfections are due to the fact that, in reality, the breakeven rate of inflation is a mix of a more complex set of factors, including the real yield on the index-linked bonds, inflation expectations, and the risk premium investors demand for holding conventional bonds in an inflationary period. Since two of these three parameters cannot be fixed with any precision, the market tends to adopt the simpler method of calculation.

Part Two

Bond "Magic Numbers" – Analysis

Bond "Magic Numbers" – Analysis

The six "magic numbers" in this section take the understanding we gained of bonds in the last section a little further. They look at techniques – some simple, some more complex – that we can use to work out which bonds look the best value when we are presented with a choice of alternatives in which to invest.

It's worth pointing out at this stage that we have concentrated throughout this book on ratios and concepts that we believe ordinary investors need to grasp, but also only those ones that they are likely to meet in everyday bond and derivative investing.

In the previous section, for example, while we looked at how to calculate returns on callable and puttable bonds (because bonds like this are readily available to ordinary investors), we didn't look at extendable and retractable bonds, and on bonds with sinking funds (bonds that are repaid in installments), bonds with step-up coupons (coupon increases if issuer's credit rating is downgraded) and the like. Because it's unlikely that most private investors will meet examples of these bonds in their everyday investing, we have not covered them in this book.

Back to the numbers. As we found out before, the relationship between bonds and interest rates is absolutely vital.

These "magic numbers" fall into one of two categories.

The first follows from the fact that we can use bond yields as a tool to compare different bonds. The comparisons could be either those bonds of different maturity that originate from the same issuer, or those with similar maturities but from different issuers.

The second category is a group of measures that describe the sensitivity or otherwise of an individual bond or group of bonds to changes in the general level of rates, or the different level of sensitivity to rate changes that are inherent in the terms of a bond – its coupon, maturity date, and so on.

In the rough order in which they crop up in the next few pages, these are:

- Yield spreads – the differences between bond yields reflecting differences in bond quality. Understanding how they work is crucial to investing in any type of bond.

- The yield curve – this shows how the length of life of a bond affects its yield. Understanding where a bond sits on the yield curve, and the way the curve moves in different circumstances, is a key part of bond investing.

- Duration – this is one of the crucial concepts in bond analysis. We can look at it in two ways. Looked at one way, it is the "half-life" of the bond, the point at which the cumulative flows of cash from a series of coupons exactly equal the cumulative flows of cash from the remaining coupons and redemption proceeds.

  Looked at another way, duration is a measure of the sensitivity of a bond's price to a fixed change in yields. Either way, it is an important tool in helping us decide between two bonds with the same yield basis and maturity date, or between two different bond portfolios.

- Convexity – however you calculate it, duration isn't an exact measure of a bond's sensitivity to interest rate changes, particularly to large movements. This is because the sensitivity changes as the yield changes. Measuring convexity allows you to adjust the duration measure to get a more accurate estimation of a bond's expected price change for any given shift in yield levels.

- Basis-point values – these reduce the duration measurement to a simple measurement of the expected change in price for a single basis-point change in yield.

Once again, all of these "magic numbers" are absolutely basic to informed bond investing. They are used by the professionals, but are also relatively easy to calculate with a simple understanding of algebra and a financial calculator or spreadsheet program.

The sections that follow examine each of these six "magic numbers" in more detail. Read on to find out how to get the data you need, how to calculate them and what they mean.

Yield Spreads

The Definition

Spreads are differences in the redemption yields of bonds. They can be differences between bonds of different maturity from the same issuer or, more normally, differences between bonds of the same maturity from different issuers. They are found by simple subtraction and normally expressed in basis points (bp), where 1bp is one-hundredth of one percent.

The Formula

Spread = RY bond A − RY bond B

The Components

Redemption yield bond A – There is not much magic in this. Simply select the two bonds you wish to compare, and subtract one yield from the other. Bond A will typically be the bond with the higher yield, since it is normal to express a spread as a positive integer.

Redemption yield bond B – The redemption yield here will typically be the bond with the lower yield or, if you are comparing two bonds from the same issuer, the one with the shorter maturity date. Bond B is sometimes a benchmark, against which bond A is being compared. In this case, it will usually be a government bond with the same, or similar, maturity date.

Where's the Data?

Redemption yields – data is normally quoted on financial websites such as Bloomberg, or in financial newspapers. Alternatively, it can be worked out from first principles using the method described in Magic Number 5.

Calculating it – the Theory

Figure 9.1 shows the different numbers to be pulled from the sources described and how to use them to calculate the ratio.

Figure 9.1 Calculating the "Magic Number" for ... Yield Spreads

The government of Titan has a bond that matures in April 2009. Work out the spread between this and the equivalent US Treasury note.

The bonds' data is as follows:

	US 5-year note	Titan 5-year
Coupon (%)	3.125	5.00
Maturity date	Apr-09	Apr-09
Price	98.8594	102.376
Interest	semi-annual	semi-annual
Red. Yield (%)	3.37	4.47
Spread		110 bp
(working)		(4.47 − 3.37) × 100

The difference in yields in percentage points is multiplied by 100 to express it in basis points.

CALCULATING IT FOR
THE FRENCH AND GERMAN FIVE-YEAR BONDS

Figure 9.2 Calculating Yield Spreads for ... French and German Five-year Bonds

The figures...

The French and German governments have bonds that mature in 2009. Work out the spread between these bonds and the equivalent US Treasury note.

The bonds' data is as follows:

	US Treasury 5-year note	French 5-year BTAN	German 5-year Bund
Coupon (%)	3.125	3.50	3.25
Maturity date	Apr-09	Jan-09	Apr-09
Price	98.8594	100.77	99.53
Interest	semi-annual	semi-annual	semi-annual
Red. Yield (%)	3.37	3.32	3.35
Spread		−5	−2
(working)		(3.32 − 3.37) × 100	(3.35 − 3.37) × 100

The French BTAN has a yield five basis points less than the US Treasury note and three basis points less than the Bund.

The example provides a good illustration of why basis points are used to calculate spreads. This is because differences in yields between G7 government bonds can be very small indeed, and calculating the difference in hundredths of a percentage point means that the result is a more sensible one.

In this case, of course, French and German government bonds stand on yields that are very close together because they can be traded without running currency risk. This is because both countries are within the Euro area, are pursuing a common monetary policy and both bonds are denominated in the same currency.

WHAT IT MEANS

Spreads reflect a range of influences and can be calculated in different ways. Comparing bonds with similar maturities is, however, the most common use of spreads.

In the section on redemption yields (Magic Number 5), we introduced the concept of a government bond yield as a measurement of the risk-free rate of return. The idea is that a bond issued by a leading government – France, Germany, the UK, the USA – is extremely unlikely to default. Default means not paying interest on time or not repaying principal in full. Bonds that are effectively free of the risk of default should have a lower yield than those where there is some such risk. Their yield is termed the "risk-free rate of return".

It is, however, very important to remember that this does not mean you are guaranteed to make a profit on the bond in question. The yield on a US Treasury Bond can still rise, and its price fall, if interest rates go up. Buying a government bond at the wrong time can lead to just as painful a loss as it would if you bought a share that went down in price. The only risk that is absent is the risk that the bond's issuer will not honor the obligations inherent in the bond.

The spread between the risk-free rate of return and the yield on, say, a bond issued by a developing country or by a publicly listed company measures the market's perception of the riskiness of the bond in question. The idea is a simple one. The greater the risk of default, the more investors must be rewarded to compensate them for running that risk. Hence, there is a continuum of yields and yield spreads over the risk-free rate that reflects, among other things, the perceived risk of the issuer defaulting.

Take one example. At the time of writing, the yield on 12-year Argentine government bonds was 43.1%, a spread of 3,857 basis points over the equivalent US Treasury bond. Brazil, generally regarded as a safer bet, has a six-year government bond on a spread of just over 500 basis points (that is, five percentage points) over the comparable US Treasury bond. This shows what investors think of the relative riskiness of bonds issued by these two governments.

Riskiness can, however, be manifested in a number of ways. One is straightforward: the risk of default. The other is a little more subtle. This is the market's perception about the likely future strength or weakness of the currency in which the bond is denominated.

In the example in Figure 9.2, the German and French bonds actually sell on lower yields than the equivalent US Treasury. In other words, the spread is negative. Swiss 10-year bonds sell on yields around 170 basis points less than US Treasuries. Since no-one expects the US Treasury or indeed the Swiss government to default, it follows that the spread must be explained by other factors. The main other factor in question is the perceived future strength or weakness in the currency. Investors in this case prefer to hold the Swiss franc rather than the US dollar.

So for bonds denominated in the same currency, spreads between bonds of similar maturities from different issuers measure perceived differences in credit quality. Across currencies they measure differences in credit quality plus the perceived currency risk. Differences in spreads between government bonds of equivalent quality can only reflect differences in perceptions about currency.

Interpreting what these spreads mean is a crucial part of bond investing. Judging when spreads are out of line with reality is one of the ways in which the professionals trade in the bond market.

MAGIC NUMBER 10

Yield Curve

THE DEFINITION

The yield curve plots the redemption yields of bonds of different maturities from the same issuer, with yield on the vertical axis and years to maturity on the horizontal axis. The result is a line that, in normal circumstances, curves up from bottom left to top right. Yield curves are typically used to analyze government bond markets.

THE FORMULA

There is no formula to calculate. What is needed, however, is for the length of maturities to be calculated and plotted proportionately on the chart.

THE COMPONENTS

Redemption yield (or yield to maturity) – redemption yield is defined in Magic Number 5. It is the annualized total return from a bond, including the compounded return from the coupon, and any gain or loss that will accrue if the bond is held to maturity.

Maturity date – maturity dates are generally fixed precisely to a specific future day. For the purposes of drawing a yield curve, most individuals would simply use the nearest year or half year when working out the time to maturity. Drawing yield curves with more precision requires a convention that allows for the differing incidence of maturity dates.

A typical system might be to allocate time units in monthly intervals for the first 18 months of maturities, then quarterly up to maturities of two years, then half-yearly to three years, and annually for subsequent data points. Some financial websites abbreviate the process by simply taking a small selection of benchmark bonds (two-year, five-year, 10-year, 20-year and 30-year).

WHERE'S THE DATA?

Redemption yields – data on redemption yields can be found in financial newspapers and websites.

Maturity dates – precise maturity dates for government bonds are normally available from the websites of the issuing authority, such as the Public Debt Office in the USA, or the Debt Management Office in the UK. Financial newspapers periodically provide data like this on their price pages.

CALCULATING IT – THE THEORY

Figure 10.1 shows the different numbers to be pulled from the sources described and how to use them to calculate the yield curve. In fact, in this case, the operation is relatively easy to do using the chart function in Excel.

MAGIC NUMBERS FOR BONDS AND DERIVATIVES

Figure 10.1 Calculating the "Magic Number" for ... the Yield Curve

The government of Alpha Centauri has bonds maturing each year for the next 10 years. The table shows the yields for different maturities

Life (years)	Redemption yield (%)
1	2.66
2	3.30
3	3.55
4	3.87
5	4.17
6	4.44
7	4.65
8	4.87
9	4.93
10	5.00

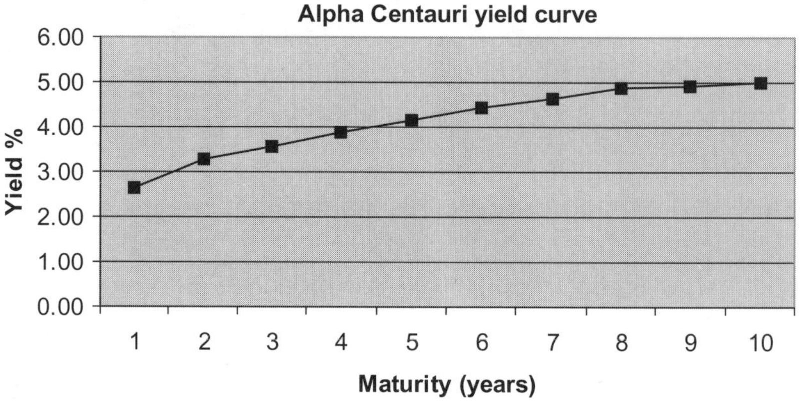

Alpha Centauri yield curve

CALCULATING IT FOR
UK GILTS

Figure 10.2 Calculating Yield Curves for UK Gilts

Life (years)	Redemption yields %	
	UKQ1 2001	UKQ1 2004
0	5.24	4.07
1	5.18	4.53
2	5.15	4.66
3	5.12	4.76
4	5.09	4.78
5	5.06	4.84
6	5.02	4.89
7	4.98	4.92
8	4.87	4.94
9	4.77	4.95
10	4.73	4.96
11		4.95
12		
13		
14	4.75	
15		
16		
17		4.92
18		
19		
20	4.61	
21		4.88
22		
23		
24		4.84
25		
26		
27	4.46	
28		4.8
29		
30		
31	4.39	
32		4.78

These two yield curves are approximately three years apart and show how yield curves can change shape over time.

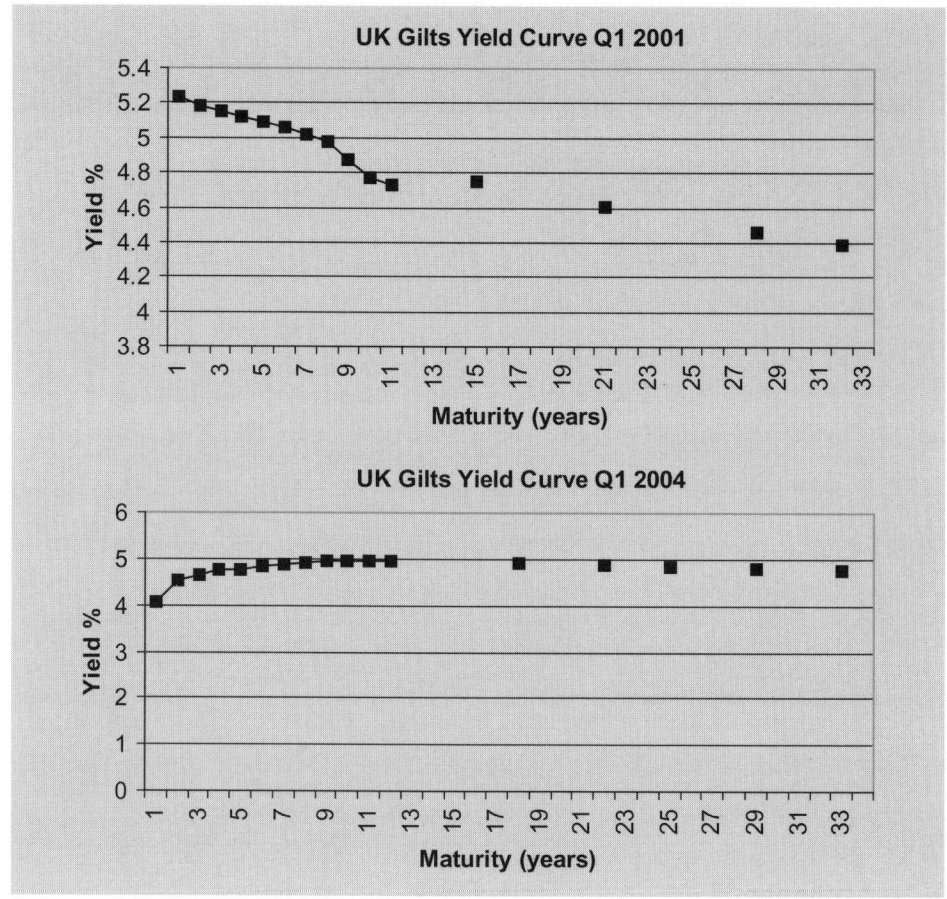

What it Means

The "time value of money" theory described in Magic Number 2 on discounting means that bonds that have longer to run to maturity normally have higher yields.

The reason for this is the simple preference of most investors for having cash now rather than cash at some point in the future. The longer we have to wait, the bigger the return we want by way of compensation.

There are several other risks you run by investing in a long-term bond rather than a shorter-term one. Not the least of these is that inflation might rise in the meantime and deplete the real value of your investment.

You can sell the bond if this happens, but you might have to take a lower price than you paid. In general terms, a bond with longer to go to maturity will show greater volatility in its price and yield than a shorter-term one. Volatility means risk, and greater risk should be rewarded with a higher return – in other words, a bigger yield.

So, in normal circumstances, for all these reasons, bonds with longer maturities should have higher redemption yields than those with a shorter time to run. In an ideal world, the increments in yield would be steadily greater as maturity lengthened. A two-year bond should yield more than a one-year bond, a five-year bond more than a two-year, a 10-year more than a five-year, and so on.

As we've described earlier, plotting redemption yield against the length of time to maturity for a range of bonds from the same issuer (say, the British government) produces the yield curve.

A normal yield curve is shown in Figure 10.1, a rounded curve sloping from bottom left to top right.

But in the real world it is rare for the yield curve to assume precisely this form. Often there may be kinks in it. It may turn up (or down) abruptly at the very short end, or the whole curve may be inverted; that is to say, instead of sloping up from left to right, it will slope the other way.

In the first quarter of 2001, the yield curve in UK government securities (gilts) looked like the top graph in Figure 10.2. In this case, short-term yields were higher than long-term ones, the reverse of what the "time value of money" would lead you to think is normal.

A curve like this is typical of a recession and, when the curve assumes such a shape, it often means that short-term interest rates will be cut to stimulate growth. This lowers yields, and raises bond prices at the "short" end of the curve. Such moves also tend to presage an improving stock market, although often there are big (and safer) gains to be made in short-term bonds as well at this time.

By Q1 2004 the yield curve in gilts had assumed a more normal shape, as shown in the lower chart in Figure 10.2.

Yield curves can move around quite sharply in some instances. For example, between October 2003 and April 2004 the yield on the UK 10-year gilt moved down from 5% to 4.6% and back up to 5% – all in the space of six months. It is currently (in early October 2004) around 4.86%.

What moves yield curves around like this is the expectation of future trends in interest rates and inflation rates. Inflation is the big enemy of long-term bondholders. This is because they are earning a fixed income the purchasing power of which, over time, will be severely depleted if inflation rises.

Interest rates, meanwhile, exert a powerful influence at the short end of the curve, because of the possibilities that investors have for switching between short-term government bonds and bank deposits. This switching, or "arbitrage", tends to mean that movements in interest rates set by central banks, or expectations of them, will "drag" the short end of the yield curve around.

Inflation expectations fix the medium and long end of the curve: short-term rates determine the very short end. The yield curve flexes between these two points. This is why the yield curve can sometimes be an important predictor of these two variables and can be used by astute bond investors as a way of picking the ideal stock to invest in at any point in time.

MAGIC NUMBER 11

Duration

THE DEFINITION

Duration is a tool to measure the sensitivity of a bond's price to hypothetical changes in the yield basis, particularly to small variations in it. There are several ways of calculating it. The one most commonly used in the bond market is known as "modified duration". The starting point is the bond's price at a given level of yield to maturity. The price is then recalculated for a small downward change in yield and for an identical upward change in yield. By a small change we mean a tenth or a quarter of one percentage point.

We then divide the difference between these two hypothetical prices by the original price multiplied by the hypothetical change in yield expressed as a decimal. This definition provides the approximate percentage price change expected in the bond for the given change in yield.

The reason for using this "magic number" is that it allows us to distinguish between two bonds that may have similar maturity dates and yields. If they have different coupons, they will have different duration percentages. Duration also allows us to measure the sensitivity of a bond portfolio, not just a single bond, to changes in the general level of yields.

THE FORMULA

Using this definition, we can get the formula:

$$D = (P_{y-} - P_{y+})/(2 \times P \times d_y)$$

Where:

D = modified duration

P_{y-} = bond price if yield falls

P_{y+} = bond price if yield rises

P = original price of bond

d_y = hypothetical change in yield expressed as a decimal

THE COMPONENTS

Bond price if yield falls – the new price implied by shifting the yield to maturity of the bond down by the specified hypothetical amount from its current yield to maturity.

Bond price if yield rises – the new price implied by shifting the yield to maturity of the bond up by the specified hypothetical amount from its current yield to maturity.

Original price of bond – the current market price of the bond.

Hypothetical change in yield – the hypothetical change in yield assumed in the calculation. The norm is to assume a fraction of one percentage point and express it in decimal point.

WHERE'S THE DATA?

Bond price if yield falls – this is calculated using the bond worksheet on a normal financial calculator: entering the terms of the bond, entering a new yield, reduced by the assumed hypothetical amount, and computing the new price.

Bond price if yield rises – this is calculated using the bond worksheet on a normal financial calculator: entering the terms of the bond, entering a new yield, increased by the assumed hypothetical amount, and computing the new price.

Original price of bond – this is found from a financial website or financial newspaper.

Hypothetical change in yield – this is assumed by the investor or the person performing the calculation.

CALCULATING IT – THE THEORY

Figure 11.1 shows the different numbers to be pulled from the sources outlined above and how to use them to calculate the ratio.

Figure 11.1 Calculating the "Magic Number" for ... Modified Duration

Pluto Widgets has issued a bond with the following terms:

Coupon 6%
Redemption date .... 31st December, 2009
Settlement date .... 30th March, 2005
Interest payments .... Semi-annual
Current price 103
Current yield to maturity 5.28%

Calculate duration for a 25-basis-point movement in yield.
Using a financial calculator, we can work out the price that would give, respectively:

A yield to maturity of 5.03% (25 bp less than the current yield) **104.05**
A yield to maturity of 5.53% (25 bp more than the current yield) **101.93**

Substituting these in the formula from the earlier part of this section:

$D = (P_{y-} - P_{y+})/(2 \times P \times d_y)$

... gives the following result:

Duration is **4.1165**
(working) $(104.05 - 101.93)/(2 \times 103 \times 0.0025)$
                                                (or $2.12/0.515$)

This is the expected percentage change in the price of the bond for a 100-basis-point change in the yield basis.

CALCULATING IT FOR
EUROPEAN INVESTMENT BANK

Figure 11.2 Calculating Duration for ... the EIB 5.625% 2032

The European Investment Bank recently issued a bond with the following terms:

Coupon 5.625%
Redemption date .... 7th June, 2032
Settlement date .... 21st April, 2004
Interest payments .... Annual
Current price 107.7
Current yield to maturity 5.10%

Calculate duration for a 25-basis-point movement in yield.

Using a financial calculator, we can work out the price that would give, respectively:

A yield to maturity of 4.85% (25 bp less than the current yield) **111.75**
A yield to maturity of 5.35% (25 bp more than the current yield) **103.94**

Substituting these in the formula from the earlier part of this section:

$D = (P_{y-} - P_{y+})/(2 \times P \times d_y)$

... gives the following result:
Duration is **14.503**
(working) $(111.75 - 103.94)/(2 \times 107.7 \times 0.0025)$
                                                         (or $7.81/0.5385$)

A one-percentage-point movement in yields will affect the price by 14.5%.

What it Means

Duration is a measurement of the sensitivity of a bond to a change in the general yield basis on which bonds are assessed. Such a change in the yield basis can come with a change in interest rates or, on longer-dated bonds, with a change in inflation expectations.

Duration is primarily related to two variables. One is the coupon paid on the bond; the other is the length of time to maturity. Other things being equal, the higher the coupon, the lower the duration, and vice versa. And other things being equal, the longer the maturity, the higher the duration, and vice versa.

Duration is in fact related to the speed with which cash comes in from owning the bond. There is a theoretically correct, if rather long-winded, way of calculating duration, which is to discount each successive coupon received by a discount rate that approximates to the current risk-free rate of return. You then work out the cumulative total of these discounted receipts. The next step is to find the point, starting from the present, at which the cumulative discounted cash flows already received exactly equal the present value of those remaining at that point. Remember, of course, that this figure will include the present value of the repayment of principal at the end of the bond's life.

Using this method of calculation, duration is expressed in years, and will be less than the remaining time left until the bond matures. There is one exception to this, which is the case of a zero-coupon bond. Here length of time to maturity and duration will be one and the same, because all of the cash flow from the bond is received in one lump sum on the day the bond is redeemed.

Using the method described in the formula above, however, provides a good approximation of this number.

There are a number of uses for duration. One is to predict price changes; another is to compare the relative sensitivity of different portfolios or categories of bonds.

Percentage changes in the price (to be accurate, in the "dirty price" of the bond) can be predicted from duration by using the formula:

Percentage price change $= - D \times d_y \times 100$

There is a minus in front of duration (D) because bond prices move inversely to yields. The expression d_y is the projected change in yield basis expressed as a decimal.

So in the case of the EIB bond used in Figure 11.2, the impact of a 10-basis point increase in yield would be: $-14.503 \times (+0.001) \times 100$, which equals -1.4503%.

We can see from this too that, if interest rates are expected to rise, it makes sense to hold bonds with short durations, since this will minimize the impact on the value of a portfolio of bonds from the adverse shift in the yield basis. The reverse is true if rates are expected to fall. If this happens, bonds with longer duration will perform better than those of short duration.

Portfolio duration is calculated simply by weighting the duration for each individual bond by the percentage it represents of the portfolio. As Figure 11.3 shows, it's possible to have duration measures for a category of bonds (in this case UK gilts), and for a bond market as a whole.

Figure 11.3 Average Duration on UK Government Bonds in April 2004

Maturity Spectrum (yrs)	Duration	Weighting
0 to 5	2.99	38.60
5 to 10	5.96	17.00
10 to 15	8.42	15.00
5 to 15	7.11	32.00
Over 15	13.44	28.80
Irredeemable	20.79	0.60
Total market	7.79	100.00

Source: Financial Times.

There are other ways of measuring duration, however, which approximate more closely to its theoretical definition. These are shown in Magic Number 12.

MAGIC NUMBER 12

Macaulay Duration

THE DEFINITION

As we outlined at the end of the previous section, the theoretically correct way of calculating duration is by discounting each successive coupon received by a discount rate equivalent to the bond's current yield to maturity.

We then find the point, measuring from the present in years and fractions of a year, at which the cumulative discounted cash flows already received exactly equal the present value of those remaining at that point, including the present value of the repayment of principal at the end of the bond's life.

Let's just use a brief example to explain this. Take a five-year bond with annual interest. Multiply each successive discounted receipt by the year in which it is received, and then divide the result by the number of years multiplied by the price. This gives the Macaulay duration figure.

There is, however, an easier way of arriving at the correct answer by using the modified duration "magic number" found in the previous section.

THE FORMULA

Full calculation

For coupon paid annually:

$$D = [(1 \times PV1) + (2 \times PV2) + (3 \times PV3) \ldots\ldots (n \times PVn)]/\text{Price}$$

For coupon paid semi-annually:

$$D = [(1 \times PV1) + (2 \times PV2) + (3 \times PV3) \ldots\ldots + (n \times PVn)]/2 \times \text{Price}$$

In these formulas we adopt the same conventions as earlier, where PV1 to PVn represent successive discounted coupon payments and, in the case of PVn, the discounted final coupon plus the principal amount repaid at the redemption price. The letter n represents the number of coupon payments.

Quick calculation

The quick way of calculating Macaulay duration is shown by the formula below.

For coupon paid annually:

Macaulay duration = Modified duration × (1 + decimal yield)

For coupon paid semi-annually:

Macaulay duration = Modified duration × (1 + 0.5 of decimal yield)

This is almost as accurate and much easier to arrive at.

The Components

Discount rate – the discount rate used, by convention, is the redemption yield on the bond itself.

Coupon frequency and rate – the coupon rate is known and the coupon frequency can generally be assumed to be either annual or semi-annual. US and UK government bonds pay interest semi-annually, and Eurobonds and European government bonds annually.

Price – the market price of the bond.

Modified duration (for quick calculation) – this is the number calculated in Magic Number 11.

Where's the Data?

Discount rate – the redemption yield on the bond can be worked out from first principles using a financial calculator, or simply taken from a financial newspaper or website.

Coupon frequency and rate – this is obtainable from the prospectus accompanying the bond issue or direct from the issuer, perhaps via their own website.

Price – the market price of the bond is quoted in financial newspapers and some financial websites. Bondscape (www.bondscape.net) carries a wide range of government and corporate bond prices.

Modified duration (for quick calculation) – this is the number calculated in Magic Number 11 and can be derived from the formula recorded there.

Calculating it – the Theory

Figure 12.1 shows the different numbers to be pulled from the sources outlined above and how to use them to calculate the ratio.

Figure 12.1 Calculating the "Magic Number" for ... Macaulay Duration

The Bank of Betelgeuse has issued a bond with the following terms:

Coupon	5%
Redemption date	31st December, 2009
Settlement date	31st December, 2004
Interest payments	Annual
Current price	103
Current yield to maturity	4.32%

To calculate Macaulay duration from first principles, we can draw up a schedule of cash flows.

Date	Type	Receipt	Disc. Adj	PV	Weight	Weighted PV
Dec-05	C	5	0.9568	4.7840	1	4.784
Dec-06	C	5	0.9155	4.5775	2	9.155
Dec-07	C	5	0.8759	4.3795	3	13.139
Dec-08	C	5	0.8381	4.1905	4	16.762
Dec-09	C+P	105	0.8019	84.1995	5	420.998
Total of weighted present values						464.838

Macaulay duration is	**4.51**
(working)	(464.84/103)
Using the formula in Magic Number 10 gives modified duration as	4.369
Macaulay duration is approximately equal to modified duration × 1 + yield	4.557
(working)	(4.369 × 1.0432)

CALCULATING IT FOR
EUROPEAN INVESTMENT BANK

Figure 12.2 Calculating Macaulay Duration for ... EIB 5.625% 2032

Because this bond's maturity date is so far out in the future, it is clearly impractical to calculate Macaulay duration from first principles. We can, however, use the quick calculation shown earlier in this section.

As a recap from the bottom half of Figure 11.2, the modifed duration is calculated as follows:

Current yield to maturity   **5.10%**

Calculate duration for 25-basis-point movement in yield.

Using a financial calculator, we can work out the price that would give, respectively:

A yield to maturity of 4.85% (25 bp less than the current yield)   **111.75**
A yield to maturity of 5.35% (25 bp more than the current yield)   **103.94**

Substituting these in the formula from the earlier part of this section:

$D = (P_{y-} - P_{y+})/(2 \times P \times d_y)$

... gives the following result:

Modified duration is... **14.503**
(working) $(111.75 - 103.94)/(2 \times 107.7 \times 0.0025)$
                                                        (or 7.81/0.5385)

From this we can use the formula:

Macaulay duration is approximately equal to modified duration $\times (1 + \text{yield})$. This gives the result:

Macaulay duration for the EIB 5.625% 2032 is: **15.243**
(working) (14.503×1.051)

WHAT IT MEANS

The arguments for using duration were rehearsed in Magic Number 11.

It is clear, however, that Macaulay duration is, strictly speaking, the more accurate of the two measures. While the quick method of calculation is generally good enough for most purposes, it is not an exact match. Having said that, of course, it's worth noting that in calculating the discount factors in Figure 11.1, we did round the discount factors to three decimal places and calculating these more accurately might have reduced the disparity between the two figures.

It is important to remember also that duration as a measure, however it is calculated, is far from being an accurate representation of the expected price change in a bond for a given change yield. For that, we need to make an adjustment to a bond's duration to reflect the convexity of the relationship between its price and yield.

How to do this is covered in Magic Number 14. But before that, we need to look at another analytical tool, namely basis-point value. This is covered in the next section.

MAGIC NUMBER 13

Basis-point Value

THE DEFINITION

Basis points are, as we explained earlier, one-hundredths of one percentage point. They are so called because they are used to measure the tiny differences in yields, known as a "basis" (or "spread"), that can be very small fractions of a percentage point.

While we might think of duration, as explained in Magic Numbers 11 and 12, as a measure of what might happen to a bond's price in the event of, say, a one-percentage-point shift in the general level of yields, in reality bond investors are often dealing in much smaller movements in yields. They also want to know the change that results from this in money terms rather than as a percentage. Basis-point value achieves this for them. It expresses duration as a decimal and multiplies it by the bond's "dirty" price expressed divided by 100. These two expressions effectively reduce the duration measurement from a one-percentage-point movement to a one-basis-point movement (that is, one-hundredth of the size), and provide the result in money rather than percentage terms.

THE FORMULA

$$BPV = (MD/100) \times (DP/100)$$

In the formula

MD = modified duration

DP = "dirty" price (that is, market price + accrued interest)

The Components

Modified duration – a tool to measure the sensitivity of a bond's price to hypothetical changes in yields, particularly to small variations in them (see Magic Number 10). The one most commonly used in the bond market is known as "modified duration". The starting point is the bond's price at a given level of yield to maturity. The price is then recalculated for a small downward change in yield and for an identical upward change in yield.

The difference between these two hypothetical prices is then divided by the original price multiplied by the hypothetical change in yield expressed as a decimal. This definition provides the approximate percentage price change expected for the given change in yield.

Market price – this is self-explanatory – the price of the bond as quoted in the market. Market prices are "clean" prices; that is, they exclude any accrued interest. Accrued interest has to be added back to arrive at the "dirty" price that we require for this calculation.

Accrued interest – the interest that has accrued on the bond since the last interest payment date and calculated according to particular market conventions (see Magic Number 3). You calculate it by pro-rating the coupon for the proportion that the number of elapsed days represents of the coupon payment period as a whole.

Where's the Data?

Modified duration – duration for bonds that are actively traded is sometimes shown in newspapers and financial websites. It can be calculated from first principles using a financial calculator by re-computing a bond's price for small identical upward and downward movements in yield and then applying the formula contained in Magic Number 10.

Market Price – this is obtainable from financial newspapers, or websites such as Bondscape (www.bondscape.net).

Accrued interest – this can be worked out from first principles using a diary to calculate days from dates and then applying the appropriate accrued interest convention (see Figure 3.3). However, most financial calculators will calculate and show accrued interest automatically as part of the process of calculating a redemption yield.

CALCULATING IT – THE THEORY

Figure 13.1 shows the different numbers to be pulled from the sources described and how to use them to calculate the ratio.

Figure 13.1 Calculating the "Magic Number" for ... Basis-point Value

In Figure 11.1 we calculated modified duration for a Pluto Widgets bond with the terms set out below.

Let's now move on from this calculation to work the BPV for the same bond.

Coupon 6%
Redemption date .... 31st December, 2009
Settlement date .... 30th March, 2005
Interest payments .... Semi-annual
Current price 103
Current yield to maturity 5.28%

Duration was 4.1165

To calculate BPV we need to work out accrued interest to arrive at the "dirty" price.

As a by-product of calculating redemption yield we arrive at the accrued interest amount, which is roughly one-quarter of the annual coupon.

Accrued interest is 1.48
So "dirty" price is   104.48
(working)   (103.00 + 1.48)

BPV is 0.043009
(working)   (0.041165 × 1.0448)

This is the duration percentage expressed as a decimal times the "dirty" price expressed as a decimal.

Calculating it for WAL-MART

Figure 13.2 Calculating Basis-point Value for the Wal-Mart 6.875% 2009

The figures ...

Wal-Mart has a US-dollar bond in issue with the following terms:

Coupon	6.875%
Coupon frequency	Semi-annual
Maturity date	10th August, 2009
Current price (date)	113.12 (22nd April, 2004)
Current yield to maturity	4.10
Price if yield 10 bp higher	112.59
Price if yield 10 bp lower	113.61

The calculations ...

Modified duration	4.5084
(working)	$(113.61 - 112.59)/(2 \times 113.12 \times 0.001)$
Accrued interest	1.36
(working)	(automatic in financial calculator)
"Dirty" price	114.48
(working)	$(113.12 + 1.36)$
BPV is	**0.05161**
(working)	(0.045084×1.1448)

The Wal-Mart bond's duration expressed as a decimal multiplied by "dirty" price expressed as a decimal.

If yield falls by one basis point, the price of the bond will rise by 5.16 cents.

What it Means

BPV is simply a useful ready-reckoner for working out the likely change in a bond's price for very small increases or decreases in yield.

Paradoxically, because the numbers are so small, market practitioners sometimes quote them 100 times larger than they actually are. Since the whole point of calculating basis-point values is to do the reverse, to work out small price movements from small yield movements, this might seem contrary.

But in many ways it makes sense. To use the example of the Wal-Mart bond in Figure 13.2 to illustrate the point, a trader might describe the BPV for the Wal-Mart bond as "five ticks" or five cents, rather than 0.05. It means the same thing, and it is easier for everyone to understand.

MAG1C NUM8ER 14
Convexity and Convexity Adjustment

THE DEFINITION

In the three previous sections we saw how duration can be used to predict changes in price for small changes in the yield basis. This helps investors to see how bond prices might react, for example, to changes in interest rates.

If we want to look at anything other than the smallest changes in yield, however, we need to adjust for the fact that the relationship between price and yield to maturity is not a simple straight line. Plotting ever-increasing redemption yields on a horizontal axis against the resulting implied price on the vertical axis normally produces a convex curve.

Perhaps the best way of illustrating this is by simply looking at relative changes in prices and yields. In the Wal-Mart example in Figure 13.2, for instance, imagine that the price increases by 1%. Recalculating the yield for the new price, we find it has dropped by 5.4% from its previous value. If we reduce the price by 1%, the yield increases by about 5.4% from its previous value.

Now imagine the calculation of duration that we used in the previous sections as a straight-line tangent that touches that convex price/yield curve at just one point, the particular intersection of price and yield at which we performed the calculation (see Figure 14.1). It follows that as we move up or down the convex price/yield relationship from the point at which the two lines touch, there will be an increasing gap between the tangent and the convex curve.

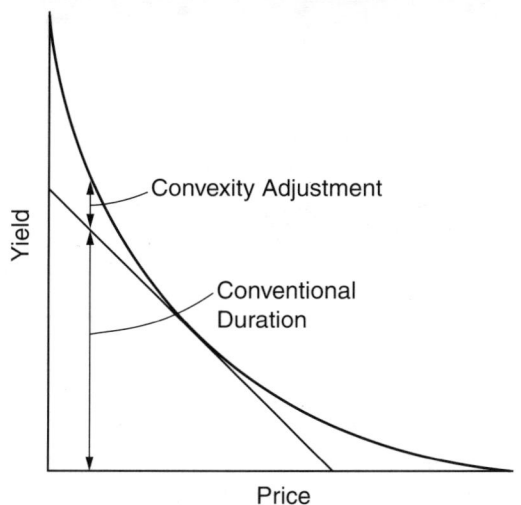

Figure 14.1 Adjusting Duration for the Curved Relationship between Price and Yield

In order to estimate the relationship between price and yield accurately, we therefore need to make an adjustment to duration to allow for the impact of convexity. Fortunately, we can derive this easily from the parameters we already have for calculating modified duration. The convexity measure is shown in the formula below.

THE FORMULA
Convexity measure

$$C = [P_{y+} + P_{y-} - 2P] / [2 \times P \times (d_y)^2]$$

Where:

P_y = bond price if yield falls by a fixed amount

P_{y+} = bond price if yield rises by the same fixed amount

P = original price of bond

d_y = hypothetical fixed change in yield expressed as a decimal

Convexity adjustment

The convexity adjustment to the percentage price change calculated by using duration is found by the following formula:

$$CA = C \times (d_y)^2 \times 100$$

This is, in effect, the gap between the tangent and the curve as described above. The norm is for the adjustment to damp down a percentage price fall resulting from a sharp upward shift in yield, and to exaggerate the percentage price rise resulting from a sharp downward shift in yield.

Convexity varies from bond to bond as a function of coupon. Low-coupon bonds have more pronounced convexity and high-coupon bonds have less pronounced convexity. Zero-coupon bonds have the most pronounced convexity.

THE COMPONENTS

The components of this equation are easy enough to understand. They are very similar to those we used in calculating modified duration in Magic Number 11.

Bond price if yield falls – the new price implied by shifting the yield to maturity of the bond down by the specified hypothetical amount from its current yield to maturity.

Bond price if yield rises – the new price implied by shifting the yield to maturity of the bond up by the specified hypothetical amount from its current yield to maturity.

Original price of bond – the current market price of the bond.

Hypothetical change in yield – the hypothetical change in yield assumed in the calculation. The norm is to assume a fraction of one percentage point.

WHERE'S THE DATA?

Bond price if yield falls – this is calculated using the bond worksheet on a normal financial calculator: entering the terms of the bond, entering a new yield, reduced by the assumed hypothetical amount, and computing the new price.

Bond price if yield rises – this is calculated using the bond worksheet on a normal financial calculator: entering the terms of the bond, entering a new yield, increased by the assumed hypothetical amount, and computing the new price.

Original price of bond – this is found from a financial website or financial newspaper.

Hypothetical change in yield – this is assumed by the investor or the person performing the calculation.

Calculating it – the Theory

Figure 14.2 shows the different numbers to be pulled from the sources described and how to use them to calculate the ratio.

Figure 14.2 Calculating the "Magic Number" for ... Convexity Adjustment

Pluto Widgets has issued a bond with the following terms:
Coupon 6%
Redemption date .... 31st December, 2009
Today's date .... 30th March, 2005
Interest payments .... Semi-annual
Current price 103
Current yield to maturity 5.28%

Calculate duration for a 25-basis-point movement in yield.

Using a financial calculator, we can work out the price that would give, respectively:

A yield to maturity of 4.28% (100 bp less than the current yield)	**107.32**
A yield to maturity of 6.28% (100 bp more than the current yield)	**98.85**
From Figure 11.1 we know that modified duration is:	4.1165

To work out convexity, we simply manipulate the price data in a different way according the formula:

$C = (P_{y+} + P_{y-} - 2P) / (2 \times P \times (d_y)^2)$

The numerator of this equation is	0.17
(working)	(107.32 + 98.85 − 206.00)
The denominator is:	0.0206
(working)	(206 × 0.0001)
The convexity measure is:	**8.25**
(working)	(0.17/0.0206)

In percentage terms, the convexity adjustment is as shown by the following formula:

$CA = C \times (d_y)^2 \times 100$

The convexity adjustment to duration is:	**0.0825%**
	(8.25 × 0.0001 × 100)

Combining duration and convexity, we can see that whereas a 100-basis-point rise in yields would result in a drop in price of 4.1165%, adjusting for convexity limits the fall to 4.034% worked out as follows: (−4.1165 + 0.0825).

A 100-basis-point fall in yields would give a percentage rise in price of 4.199% when the convexity adjustment is added to the duration measure.

CALCULATING IT FOR
WAL-MART

> **Figure 14.3 Calculating Convexity Adjustment for the Wal-Mart 6.875% 2009**
>
> **The figures ...**
>
> As we found in Magic Number 13, Wal-Mart has a US-dollar bond in issue with the following terms:
>
> Coupon 6.875%
> Coupon frequency .... Semi-annual
> Maturity date .... 10th August, 2009
> Current price (date) .... 113.12 (22nd April, 2004)
> Current yield to maturity 4.10
> Price if yield 100 bp higher 108.15
> Price if yield 100 bp lower 118.32
> Modified duration (from Figure 13.2) 4.5084
>
> As above, to work out convexity we simply manipulate the price data in a different way according the formula:
>
> $C = (P_{y+} + P_{y-} - 2P) / (2 \times P \times (d_y)^2)$
>
> The numerator of this equation is 0.23
> (working) $(118.32 + 108.15 - 226.24)$
> The denominator is: 0.022624
> (working) (226.24×0.0001)
>
> **The convexity measure is:** **10.166**
> (working) $(0.23 / 0.022624)$
>
> In percentage terms, the convexity adjustment is as shown by the following formula:
>
> $CA = C \times (d_y)^2 \times 100$
>
> **The convexity adjustment to duration is:** **0.1017%**
> $(10.166 \times 0.0001 \times 100)$
>
> Combining duration (4.5084) and convexity, we can see that whereas a 100-basis-point rise in yields would result in a drop in price of 4.5084%, adjusting for convexity limits the fall to 4.4067% worked out as follows: $(-4.5084 + 0.1017)$.
>
> A 100-basis-point fall in yields would produce a percentage rise in price of 4.6101% when the convexity adjustment is added to the duration measure.

What it Means

Calculating duration is a relatively easy process with a financial calculator and a piece of paper, and well worth doing to get to know the basic properties of a bond you might be thinking of buying. You can also use it to compare two bonds that have ostensibly similar maturities and yields.

Is convexity an overly complex step too far? It really depends on the type of bond you are buying, the amount of cash you are planning to invest in it, and the time horizon you are adopting. Clearly, convexity is particularly important if you are thinking of buying a zero-coupon bond, because this is where convexity is at its maximum. For high-coupon bonds where convexity is low, or if you are buying a bond strictly for the long term, or primarily for its income, then convexity may not matter so much to you.

Traders who use convexity calculations have it calculated for them by their professional trading-screen services such as Bloomberg and Reuters. Private investors need to use either an online calculator of the sort available at sites such as Investopedia.com, or write their own spreadsheet routines to do the calculations quickly from the yield inputs from a financial calculator.

One final point is that convexity calculations can get slightly more complex when more complex bonds are involved, particularly those with call or put features. These are when the issuer may have the option to redeem the bond early under certain circumstances, or where the holder of the bond can opt to redeem.

These are not uncommon features, and we covered how to calculate the yields on bonds like this in Magic Number 7. The presence of what amounts to an embedded option in the bond affects the shape of the price/yield relationship and can mean that the bond has negative convexity at certain price and yield combinations.

These quirks can be incorporated in the formula for convexity adjustment but, in circumstances like this, you need to pay particular attention to the correct algebraic use of plus and minus signs to work out the adjustments.

Last of all, remember that strictly speaking the percentage price changes predicted by duration and convexity measure the change to the "dirty" price of the bond.

Part Three

Futures and Options "Magic Numbers"

Futures and Options "Magic Numbers"

The eight "magic numbers" that follow look at some of the basic parameters that investors need to understand before they begin using derivatives such as futures and options. Most of them relate to options. Futures are relatively simple products, although not that easy to trade profitably. Options are more complex, and need more analysis.

Central to both types of derivatives is the concept of *volatility*, so we give this pride of place. The volatility in the price of the underlying security, index or bond on which the derivative is based is crucial.

With futures, which are, in effect, traded using a small upfront deposit known as margin, the volatility of the "underlying" governs the percentage size of the security deposit a trader has to put up.

A government bond generally has low volatility, so derivatives based on these can be bought and sold with only a small percentage (maybe 5% of the contract's value) being paid upfront. Futures on more volatile instruments, such as commodities, stock market indices and shares, demand higher upfront margin percentages.

A future can be ascribed a theoretical value, and Magic Number 16 shows how to calculate it. Because you don't have to put up the full underlying value to trade it, there is a theoretical interest saving over an equivalent purchase of the underlying security or index. This is the main reason why the *fair value of a future* will differ for any value of the underlying.

The *fair value on an option*, which we show in Magic Number 17, depends on a range of factors, and we show what they are and how they interrelate. Crucial to an option's value is the understanding of the *time value and intrinsic value* components of the option's price, and whether the option is "in the money", "at the money" or "out of the money". We show how to calculate this.

The following two sections look at the "Greeks". This is shorthand for the sensitivity of the option price to a range of variables, including the price of the underlying security, its volatility, the passage of time, the prevailing rate of interest, and so on. These numbers all tell us important things about how the price of the option will behave as markets change.

Finally we look at two concepts that are also important when using options. *Static and if-called returns* look at how to evaluate covered calls, regarded by many as one of the best-kept money-making secrets in the options market. And, last of all, market professionals often use the *put–call ratio* to gauge sentiment in the wider market as a whole.

As in the previous two parts of this book, we think that these "magic numbers" are all absolutely basic to informed investing using futures and options. They are all used by the professionals, but relatively easy to calculate. You can work them out with a simple understanding of algebra, a financial calculator or spreadsheet program, and a computerized option-valuation model. Many valuation models like this are available free of charge on the web, or for download to your computer. Some locations for such models are shown in the Appendix.

The sections that follow examine each of these eight "magic numbers" and "magic number" groups in more detail. Read on to find out how to get the data you need, how to calculate them, and what they mean.

MAG1C NUM8ER 15

Volatility

THE DEFINITION

Volatility is a statistical measure of fluctuations in the price of a share, a market index or the value of any asset. It is generally taken to be a proxy for risk. The higher the volatility of an asset, the greater is the chance of losing money when trading it. Volatility fluctuates over time. It is a key component of option prices and for calculating margin on futures contracts, which is the reason for looking at it here.

THE FORMULA AND ITS COMPONENTS

Volatility equates to the percentage standard deviation of the price of a stock, index or other asset. Standard deviation is a statistical term. It measures the degree of dispersion from a "line of best fit" calculated using regression analysis. To find it, we calculate the arithmetic average of a series of numbers and then subtract each number from the average to give the "distance" from it. We then square each of these differences, add up the result, and divide this total by the number of values we have minus one. We can then take the square root of the result to get standard deviation.

In other words:

$$SD^2 = \text{sum of } (X - Xa)^2 / n - 1$$

Where:

SD = standard deviation

X = a number (i.e. a price or index value)

Xa = average of n numbers

The percentage volatility is then given by:

$V = SD \times 100 / Xa$

or, in other words, the percentage the standard deviation represents of the previously calculated average.

The calculation can usually be performed using a series of prices over the timescale required and the statistical functions available in Excel.

However, while this seems convoluted, there is a quick way of estimating volatility, as follows:

Volatility = [(period high − period low)/2] × 100/current share price

In other words, take half of the difference between the high and low for the period in question and express it as a percentage of the share price (or, strictly speaking, the average share price) over the same period.

Volatility can be calculated over any period of time. The time period used should correspond to the maximum time over which you are likely to hold the asset in question.

WHERE'S THE DATA?

Share price data – You can find share, index or asset price information, including 52-week highs/lows, in the pages of a financial newspaper. Many investment software packages contain a means of accessing daily share price data for individual shares and indices.

Because volatility is a key component of option prices, some options exchanges supply indicative volatility data for the shares and indices in which they have listed options. As we will find later, volatility can also be calculated from software used to value options.

CALCULATING IT – THE THEORY

Figure 15.1 shows the different numbers required and how to use them to estimate volatility.

Figure 15.1 Calculating the "Magic Number" for ... Volatility

Venusian Widgets Inc. has share price information as follows:

In the six months to December 2000
Average share price was.. $20
High–low over the period was $27–17

Volatility can be estimated as.. 25%
(working) $[(27 - 17)/2] \times 100/20$

In other words, the difference between the high and low (10) divided by 2 (= 5) as a percentage of the price.

Calculating it for
THE NIKKEI 225 AND S&P 500

Figure 15.2 shows recent highs and lows in the Nikkei 225 and S&P 500 indices, together with the current price, and how they can be used to produce the "magic number". We also compute a value for volatility using the "average" and "standard deviation" functions in Microsoft Excel as a check.

Figure 15.2 Calculating Volatility for the Nikkei and the S&P

The figures ...

	Nikkei		S&P	
	Last Year	Last Qtr	Last Year	Last Qtr
High	12,128	12,128	1,158	1,157
Low	8,036	10,365	916	1,091
Current	12,121	12,121	1,135	1,135

The calculations ...

Approximation

50% of the difference between High–low is ...	2,046	881.5	121	33
(working)	(12,128 − 8,036)/2	etc.	etc.	
This figure as a percentage of the current value is (i.e. est. volatility) is ...	16.88%	7.27%	10.66%	2.91%
(working)	(2,046 × 100)/12,121	etc.	etc.	

Using Excel functions

Check by using statistical functions in Excel	12.37%	4.82%	10.15%	1.40%
(working)	(std. dev. expressed as % of average over period)			

What it Means

The example shows that the quick method of calculation gives an approximation for volatility, but that using the first-principles method is more accurate. Fortunately, even simple option-valuation software makes it easy to estimate volatility.

Volatility is intuitively easy to grasp. Every investor knows that some shares (or indices) move around more violently than others. Equally, there are times when an individual share (or index) goes through a quiet period. Little movement may occur in its price, and then it may inexplicably explode into life.

The next step to understanding volatility is to appreciate that the more volatile a share or index, then (other things being equal) the higher the risk in holding it. The reason is obvious. The greater the volatility, the more likely it is that a move will occur while you are holding the share that will result in you showing a loss.

The complication is that past share price performance may not be a reliable guide for the future. The statistical techniques described above measure the volatility based on the past performance of a particular share or index. This is known as "historic volatility".

What a derivatives investor really wants to know, however, is not what has happened to a share in the past, but the expected future trend in volatility. Why? Because this is crucial to what happens to the price of an option. Option-pricing software allows for the calculation of volatility implied by the current market price of particular options. This is called "implied volatility". It may differ considerably from historic volatility. Equally, since it represents the market's current guess as to what volatility might be over the life of an option, it too can change rapidly as market sentiment changes.

MAGIC NUMBER 16

Fair Value of a Future

THE DEFINITION

A future is a binding agreement to buy or sell a specific quantity of a commodity, bond, share or index at the market price prevailing at a predetermined future delivery date. It is a direct substitute to owning the underlying commodity, index or other asset. If you buy and hold the future until the delivery date, you must make delivery of the underlying quantity specified in the contract at the then ruling price.

It rarely comes to that, of course. Most futures trades are "closed"; that is to say, the initial transaction is reversed and a profit or loss recorded, prior to the delivery date. But it nonetheless follows that at any point prior to the delivery date there is a strict mathematical relationship between the price of the asset on which the future is based and the price of the future.

This is related to the cost of borrowing to acquire the value inherent in the futures contract (namely the total value of its constituent parts) less the income generated by the contract's underlying constituents.

Think of it this way. Rather than buy a futures contract in the Dow Jones Index, you could borrow in order to buy and hold the 30 stocks that comprise it, until the delivery date in the contract, in the proportions they represent in the index.

By doing this, you incur interest costs, but by owning the stocks rather than the index, you receive dividends. So you can deduct this income from the borrowing costs you bear. The net figure, borrowing costs less income, is called the "net cost of carry".

Now look at the futures contract. Here you do not receive dividends, but you do get exposure to the index movement without having to borrow the full value of the contract. It's a mirror image of what we have just described. The bottom line here is that the net cost of carry for the underlying should be reflected in the difference in value between the future and the underlying.

Let's put it another way. The fair value of the future reflects the interest saving from holding the future rather than the underlying, less any income that might be forgone as a result.

What this means in practice is that the "fair value" price of the future will normally be slightly above or slightly below the actual price of the underlying asset, depending on the interplay between these factors, but will converge with this underlying (the so-called cash market) price as the delivery date approaches.

THE FORMULA

Fair value = underlying price × [1 + interest rate × (days to expiry/365)] − income received

Since you can't easily work out what dividends or other income would be paid when, in practice this formula becomes:

Fair value = underlying price × [1 + (interest rate − income yield) × (days to expiry/365)]

THE COMPONENTS

Underlying price – the price of the underlying asset or basket of assets on which the future is based. With a bond future, for example, the future's contract specification will usually designate certain bonds in particular proportion as being acceptable modes of delivery. For an index future, stock future or commodity future, the price is transparent and obvious.

Interest rate – normally the rate at which dealers will be able to finance borrowing. For the sake of argument, we can take this to mean the central bank minimum lending rate.

Income yield – income yield could be the dividend yield on a share index, the accrued income on a bond, and so on. The important point is that, if an income is paid, then some way needs to be found to reflect it in the fair-value price.

Even with single stock futures, where it is known with some precision when dividends will be paid, the amount of the expected payment is usually priced into the future by the market in the run-up to the ex-dividend date, so that this event usually barely registers on the price of the future.

Commodities generally yield no income, so this aspect will be absent from fair-value calculations for commodities futures.

Days to expiry/delivery – the number of days from the present until the delivery date specified in the futures contract.

Where's the Data?

Underlying price – is available in a financial newspaper or on a financial website.

Interest rate – is available in a financial newspaper or on a financial website. Look for the rate indicated on short-term money, such as the inter-bank rate or central bank repo rate.

Income yield – can usually be found in a financial newspaper or on a financial website.

Days to expiry/delivery – the delivery date for the future is stated in the contract specifications for the future. The difference between this date and the present, in the number of days, can be found using a days-from-dates table, or from a normal desk diary.

Calculating it – the Theory

Figure 16.1 shows the different numbers to be pulled from the sources described and how to use them to calculate this particular "magic number".

Figure 16.1 Calculating the "Magic Number" for ... Fair Value of a Future

Venusium metal futures have the following characteristics and underlying values:

Delivery date .... 17th September (day 260)
Underlying value .... V$5,000
Underlying yield 0.00%
Bank of Venus interest rate 5.75%
Today's date .... 31st March (day 90)

Calculate the fair value of the future.

$FV = 5{,}000 \times [1 + (0.0575 - 0.00) \times (260 - 90)/365]$
$FV = 5{,}000 \times [1 + 0.0575 \times 0.4657]$
$FV = 5{,}000 \times 1.026778$
$FV = 5{,}133.9$

The Venusium future, being a commodity, earns no income and so the net cost of carry equates to the Bank of Venus short-term interest rate for the period until delivery is due.

Accordingly, the fair value of the future is a V$133.9 premium to the cash-market price.

Calculating it for
FTSE 100 FUTURE

Figure 16.2 Calculating Fair Value for ... FTSE 100 Future

The figures ...

The June FTSE100 Future has the following contract specification and underlying values:

Delivery date .... 18th June (day 170)
Underlying value 4,570
Underlying yield 3.14%
UK repo rate (at time of writing) 4.00%
Today's date .... 26th April (day 117)

The calculation ...

$FV = 4,570 \times [1 + (0.04 - 0.0314) \times (170 - 117)/365]$
$FV = 4,570 \times [1 + 0.0086 \times 0.145]$
$FV = 4,570 \times 1.001247$
$FV = 4,575.7$

The fair value of the future is a 5.7-point premium to the cash-market price.

Note that the future can trade at a premium or discount to fair value, depending on supply and demand. At the time this calculation was performed, the market price of the future was 4,571, a 4.7-point discount to fair value.

This suggests the futures market expected the cash market to trade lower in the short term. In the example, the following day saw the index close at 4,571.8 and the future at 4,577.0, very near to its fair value.

What it Means

Fair value for a future reflects the interest saving from holding the future rather than the underlying, but also allows for dividends or other income that might be forgone through not holding the underlying

As we saw in the example of the FTSE 100 future in Figure 16.2, the future trades independently of both the index and of its fair value, although normally the market price of the future and its fair value will not diverge too far from each other. A big gap would allow a profitable trading opportunity to open up for arbitrageurs.

Where the future trades relative to its fair value can sometimes give an indication of the likely short-term direction of the underlying market, although the only certainty is that the gap is likely to close fairly quickly. If the future trades at, say, a five-point discount to fair value, that gap could be closed by the index heading down or by the future appreciating relative to the index, or by a combination of the two.

Options, the other main category of derivatives also have a fair value, but calculating this requires us to know rather more variables. This is covered in Magic Number 17.

MAGIC NUMBER 17

Fair Value of an Option

THE DEFINITION

An option gives the holder the right, but not the obligation, to buy (in the case of a call option) or sell (in the case of a put option) a specified quantity of a share, bond, index or other asset at a fixed exercise price at any time during its life or on the date it expires.

The fair value of an option is determined by several factors: the price volatility of the underlying asset; the price of the underlying asset relative to the exercise price of the option; the length of time remaining until expiry; whether the option is a call or a put; whether the option can be exercised at any time prior to expiry (an American-style option) or only on the expiry date (a European-style option); and the level of interest rates.

THE FORMULA

This is a difficult one. There is more than one way of pricing options. The original formula worked out for calculating option prices is known as Black-Scholes, after its devisers. Others that provide a more accurate result for some specific option types have superseded it. These improve on the original Black-Scholes model, which had some drawbacks. For example, it assumed that underlying prices moved randomly, it did not accommodate dividends and it assumed that exercise took place on a specific day. A modified Black-Scholes model was released later to rectify this failing.

Even a brief survey of option literature produces at least 14 other ways to value options, depending on the type of option being considered. The main alternative to Black-Scholes is known as the "binomial model", which allows a variety of parameters to be accommodated. These include dividend payments, early exercise, changes in interest rates during the life of the option, and so on.

Even Black-Scholes is complex. In mathematical jargon, it is a linear parabolic partial differential equation. Fortunately this formula, and the equally complex binomial model for pricing options, is readily incorporated in a wide range of free and online software products and calculators, and in some downloadable Excel add-ins.

In short, we don't need to see the actual (and rather scary) formula to be able to use it to calculate the fair value of an option.

THE COMPONENTS

Price of underlying – the market price of the asset over which the option has been granted.

Type of option – there are only two types of option: call options (options to buy) and put options (options to sell).

Exercise style – for the purposes of this book we are simply considering American-style options and European-style options. American-style options allow exercise at any time up to the expiry date. These would normally be valued using the binomial method. European-style options can be exercised only on the expiry date and can be valued using the Black-Scholes method.

Readers should be aware, however, that many other types of exercise style exist, including Bermudan options, which allow exercise on or between specific dates in the future; barrier options; quanto options; binary options; and many others.

Exercise price – the price that, if the option is exercised, the option holder will pay or receive for the underlying stock or other instrument specified in the contract. This is sometimes known as the "strike price".

Risk-free rate of return – this is necessary to value the option because those granting the option (known as "option writers") must, in theory, finance a purchase of the underlying stock to deliver at the exercise price (in the case of a call option) or have the cash available to buy the underlying stock at the exercise price (in the case of a put option). The risk-free rate of return is, therefore, a proxy for what this will cost and must therefore be incorporated in the options price.

Volatility of underlying – a crucial variable. We explored the nature of volatility more thoroughly in Magic Number 15. The reason for its importance is that high levels of volatility make exercise more likely, and therefore will also be factored into the market price of the option.

Time to expiry/expiry date – the remaining life of the option is important to any determination of price. As options near the end of their life, the element in the price that represents the chance of their being able to be exercised profitably declines progressively more quickly. Throughout the life of an option, its value, for any given price of the underlying security, will be declining for this reason. All options expire on known future dates.

WHERE'S THE DATA?

Price of underlying – in the usual place in a financial newspaper or website.

Type of option – set by the terms of the option contract. You can specify whether you buy a call or a put.

Exercise style – specified in the terms of the option contract. In practice, options on stocks are American-style; options on indices can be either American- or European-style. You can choose which exercise style you want. European-style options cost less than their American-style equivalent, other things being equal.

Exercise price – stated in the terms of the option contract. You can choose from a range of exercise prices.

Risk-free rate of return – the usual central bank minimum lending rate, available from a central bank website or a financial newspaper or website.

Volatility of underlying – can be calculated from first principles, as described in Magic Number 15. What is more normal, however, is that option-pricing models are used to calculate the volatility implied by a given option price, since the market price of the option is generally known and obtainable from options-exchange websites or the financial press.

Most option-pricing models allow the user the choice of either calculating an option's price for a given level of volatility or an option's implied volatility for a given option price.

Time to expiry/expiry date – all options expire on known future dates, set by the options exchange where they are listed. Details of these dates are available from the option exchange's website. Some options expire monthly, but most expire on the basis of a quarterly cycle.

Most option-valuation models require you to submit the time to expiry in the form of the number of days. Hence, we need to calculate the number of days from dates, much as we did for the accrued-interest calculation in Magic Number 3.

CALCULATING IT – THE THEORY

Figure 17.1 shows the different numbers to be pulled from the sources described and how to use them to calculate the "magic number".

Figure 17.1 Calculating the "Magic Number" for . . . Fair Value of an Option

The MAR100 is the stock market index for the Martian stock exchange.

There are listed options in the index. The one we want to value has the following characteristics:

Exercise price	5,000	
Price of underlying index	6,000	
Call or put?	Call	
Exercise style	European	
Expiry date	15th December	Day 349
Today's date	10th June	Day 161
Risk-free rate of return	4%	
Volatility of the index	15%	

Substituting these values in a standard options calculator produces the result shown in the first screenshot:

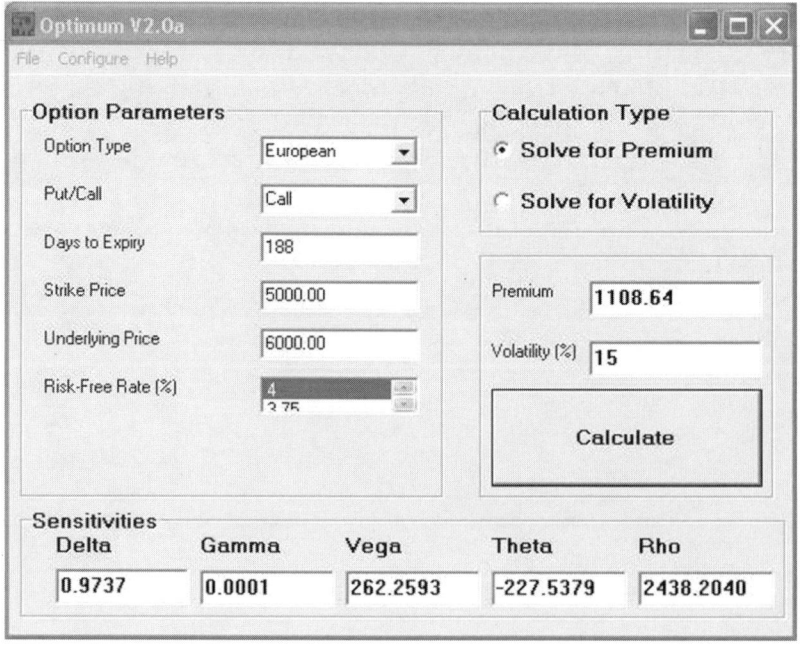

© Nigel Webb Software

In other words, this European-style call option with 188 days to expiry has a fair value of 1,108.64 based on our estimate for the historic volatility of the index.

However, let's assume that the option's price is actually 1,200. The only variable that we don't know for certain is volatility. We can input the price the market tells us the option is worth and solve the valuation to give us the implied volatility. This is shown in the second screenshot

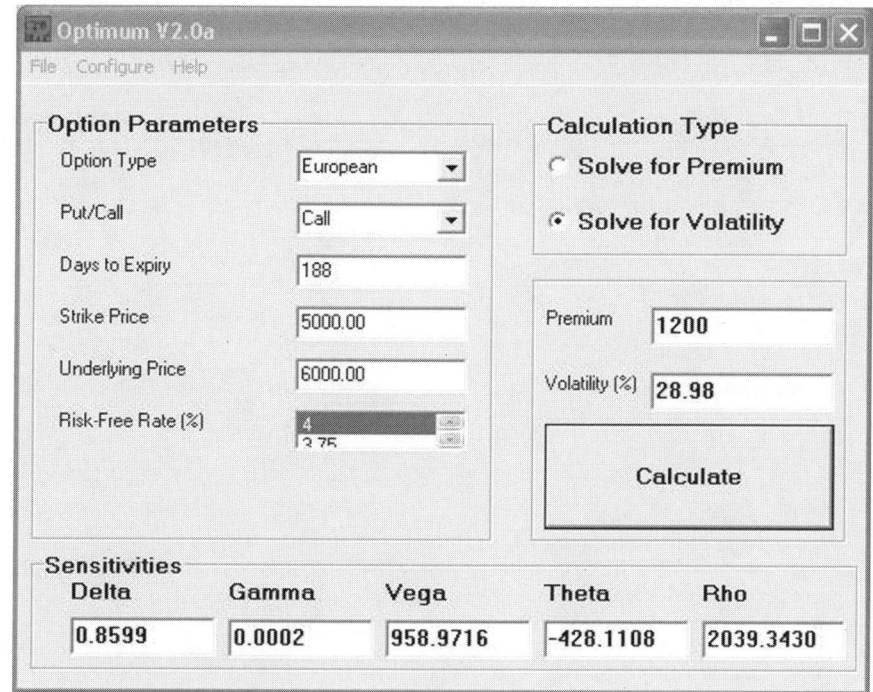

© Nigel Webb Software

This tells us that volatility implied by the option's market price is actually 29%, not the 15% we had assumed earlier.

CALCULATING IT FOR
ALTRIA OPTIONS

Figure 17.2 Calculating Fair Value for . . . Altria Options

The figures . . .

Altria (ticker symbol MO) has options listed on the Chicago Board Options Exchange (CBOE).

We think that there may be a setback in the price of the stock and want to play this by buying a put option.

The following factors are relevant:

Exercise price	$65.00	
Price of underlying shares	$55.10	
Call or put?	Put	
Exercise style	American	
Expiry date	4th September	Day 247
Today's date	29th April	Day 119
Risk-free rate of return	1%	
Option price (premium)	$11.20	
Volatility of the index	?	

Before we proceed any further, let's work out the volatility for this option, which currently has 128 days to go to expiry. This is shown in the screenshot below:

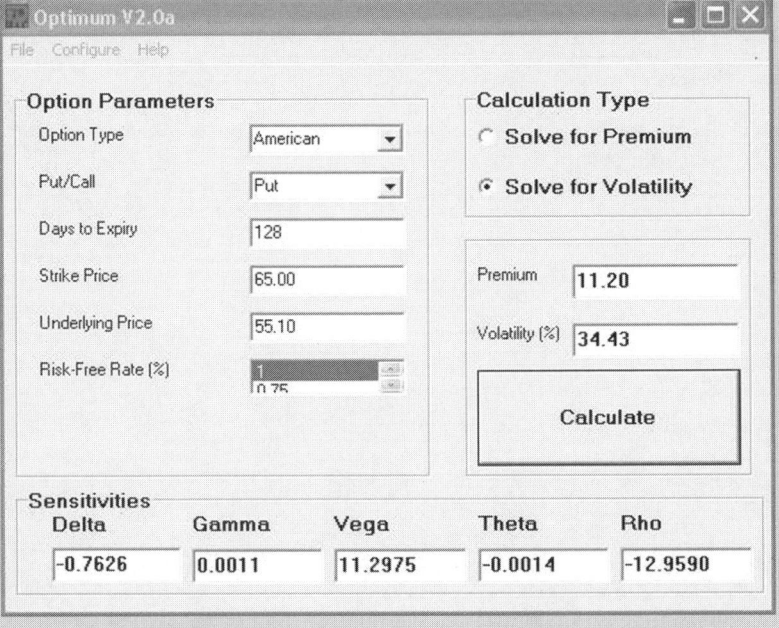

© Nigel Webb Software

Implied volatility is 34.43%.

We think the shares could drop to around $45 in two months' time and that volatility could rise to around 40%. What would this suggest for the price of the option? Plugging the new volatility number and the reduced days to expiry into the model, and solving for premium, we can work out the new fair value.

This is shown in the screenshot below:

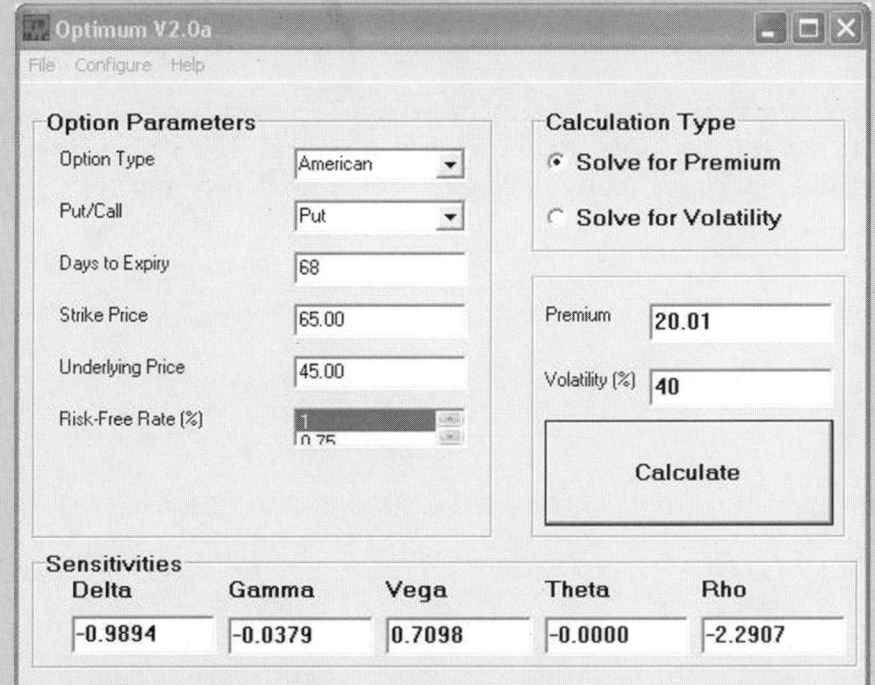

© Nigel Webb Software

If this scenario happens, the model suggests the option's price would rise from its current $11.20 to around $20.

What it Means

This series of screen shots shows exactly how we can use pricing models that calculate fair value to look for the potential upside in options trades. Typically, the swing factors affecting the value of an option are movements in the underlying price, the time to expiry and the volatility of the underlying price.

If we can envisage a scenario where volatility changes by an assumed amount, and the underlying price moves to a new level over an assumed period, then we can work out what would happen to the option price as a result.

This actually sounds more difficult than it is. Calculating the fair value of the option under this new scenario is an essential, but relatively easy, part of the process. The drawback is, of course, that if your judgment on the underlying price is incorrect you may end up losing money in the option.

Profits in options can be large when you get a trade right, but losses can be equally large when you get it wrong. The saving grace of buying options is that you cannot lose more than you invest.

MAG1C NUM8ER 18

Time Value and Intrinsic Value of an Option

THE DEFINITION

The time value of an option is the difference between the price (or premium) of an option and its intrinsic value (if any). Time value moves progressively more quickly to zero the closer an option gets to its expiry date.

The intrinsic value of an option is the extent to which the underlying price is above (in the case of a call option) or below (in the case of a put option) the exercise price of the option. Intrinsic value is either a positive integer or zero. It cannot be negative.

An option with intrinsic value is said to be "in the money". One where the underlying price and the exercise price are similar is "at the money". One where there is no intrinsic value is said to be "out of the money".

THE FORMULA

$TV = P_o - IV$

$IV_c = P_u - P_e$

$IV_p = P_e - P_u$

Where:

TV = time value

IV_c = intrinsic value of a call

IV_p = intrinsic value of a put

P_e = exercise price of option

P_o = price of option

P_u = price of underlying security

NB. IV is either positive or, if negative, written as zero.

The Components

Price of the option – the market price (or premium) of the option.

Exercise price of the option – the price at which option holders can buy (in the case of a call) or sell (in the case of a put) a fixed quantity of the underlying security should they decide to exercise their right to do so.

Price of the underlying security – the market price of the underlying security.

Where's the Data?

Price of the option – available in the usual daily financial newspapers or listed at option-exchange websites. These usually contain the prices of all options for a wide range of exercise prices and expiry dates whereas newspapers, for reasons of space, only include prices for a limited number of options.

Exercise price of the option – part of the terms of the option and usually explicitly stated along with the option price and expiry date. For example, "Widgets Inc July 500 calls" indicates a call option in the shares of Widgets Inc which expires in July and has an exercise price of 500.

Price of the underlying security – found from the usual sources, either a daily financial newspaper or financial website.

TIME VALUE AND INTRINSIC VALUE OF AN OPTION

Calculating it – the Theory

Figure 18.1 shows the different numbers to be pulled from the sources described and how to use them to calculate these parameters.

Figure 18.1 Calculating the "Magic Number" for ... Time Value and Intrinsic Value

Neptune Universal Widgets Inc. has the following options available:

Option A is a call option with a strike price of $50 and a price of $10.

Option B is a put option with a strike price of $65 and a price of $25.

Neptune Universal's stock price is currently $48.

Applying the formulas to calculate intrinsic value and time value gives the following results:

Option A

Option A intrinsic value is 0
(working)   (48 – 50 is negative and therefore read as 0)
Option A time value is $10
(working)   (10 – 0)

Option A is an out-of-the-money call. Its price is entirely represented by time value.

Option B

Option B intrinsic value is.. $17
(working)   (65 – 48)
Option B time value is $8
(working)   (25 – 17)

Option B is an in-the-money put with intrinsic value of $17. Its time value is the price of the option less this intrinsic value.

Since time value erodes to zero at expiry, another way of looking at intrinsic value is that, if the underlying price remains the same, intrinsic value will equate to the price of the option at expiry.

Calculating it for
ALTRIA

Figure 18.2 Calculating Time Value and Intrinsic Value for Altria Options

Let's take another example from Altria's listed option prices at the time of writing.

The September 45 call is priced at $10.50.

The September 45 put is priced at $0.70.

The stock is at $55.10.

The Altria September 45 Call

Intrinsic value is 10.10
(working)   (55.10 − 45.00)
Time value is 0.40
(working)   (10.50 − 10.10)

This is an in-the-money call, although time value is very low. If the underlying stock price remains the same until expiry on 4th September, the price of the option would then be $10.10.

The Altria September 45 Put

Intrinsic value is 0.00
(working)   (45.00 − 55.10 is negative and therefore read as 0)
Time value is $0.70
(working)   (0.70 − 0.00)

This is an out-of-the-money put. Time value is still low, but higher than for the equivalent call. If the price remains the same until expiry on 4th September, the option will then be worthless.

What it Means

Time value and intrinsic value are important concepts in the options market. If you are buying an out-of-the-money option, whether it is a call option or put option, its price will consist only of time value, which will erode progressively more rapidly as expiry approaches.

Of course, what buyers of such options hope and expect is that the option will move into the money before expiry and provide them with a handsome profit. What they want is volatility to rise, because this increases the chance that there will be a swing in the underlying price that will carry their option into the money and allow them to exit at a profit. In an out-of-the-money option, the gearing of returns to price movements in the underlying is that much greater.

Options with intrinsic value are rather more conservative investments. Here, the intrinsic value represents a cushion that can help insulate the option holder from minor swings in the underlying price. In this case, the gearing of the price of the option to movements in the underlying security price will be lower than for the out-of-the-money option.

Although there is still the risk that a sharp movement in the wrong direction will leave the option holder relying on time value alone, the price has to move some distance – at least by the amount of the intrinsic value – for this to happen.

One point worth bearing in mind is that buyers of options often underestimate the impact on performance of the erosion of time value. It is perfectly possible to buy an in-the-money option and yet lose money on it because the erosion of time value eliminates the potential profit you might make.

Magic Number 19 looks in more detail at the gearing inherent in options and how to measure it.

MAGIC NUM8ER 19

Delta and Gamma

THE DEFINITION

A by-product of option-valuation models is a group of ratios that are known collectively as "the Greeks", so called because they are denoted by Greek letters.

Typically these numbers explore the link between the value of the option and something that affects its value, such as the price of the underlying security, the passage of time, a change in interest rates, or a change in volatility. Here, and in Magic Number 20, we explore how they work.

Arguably one of the most important of these values is "delta". Delta provides a measure of how the price of the option reacts to a fixed change in the price of the underlying share, index or other security on which it is based. At its simplest, therefore, delta is the change in option price for a $1.00, or €1.00, or £1 (or a one-hundredth part thereof) movement in the underlying price. The delta for a call is a positive amount between 0 and 1. A put delta is a negative amount between 0 and −1, to reflect the fact that the price of a put option moves in the opposite direction to the underlying price.

Gamma is related to delta. It is the change in the *delta* for a one-unit change in the price of the underlying. This reflects the fact that the delta value changes as the price itself changes. The delta of an option that is 20p in the money will be different from one that is 30p in the money. The more in-the-money the option, the closer the delta gets to 1 (or −1 in the case of a put). The more out-of-the-money the option, the closer the delta gets to zero. Gamma measures how this relationship changes.

The Formula

Delta = Change in option value/Change in value of underlying.

In fact, the specific formulas for the delta of call and put are somewhat more complex than this, as the algebraic terms below show:

Call delta = $e^{-D(T-t)}N(d_1)$

Put delta = $e^{-D(T-t)}N(d_1) - 1$

In reality, we do not need to concern ourselves unduly with these complexities. Deltas, and the other Greeks, are worked out automatically for you by any simple option-pricing software. The important point is grasping the concept.

Looking at gamma, for example, the simple formula is:

Gamma = Change in delta value/Change in underlying value

The Components

The components that need to be pinned down are those you need to enter into an option-pricing model to establish the fair value of an option, as shown in Magic Number 17. These are:

Price of underlying – the market price of the asset over which the option has been granted.

Type of option – there are only two types of option: call options and put options.

Exercise style – for the purposes of this book we are simply considering American-style options and European-style options. American-style options allow exercise at any time up to the expiry date. These would normally be valued using the binomial method.

European-style options can be exercised only on the expiry date and would normally be valued using the Black-Scholes method.

Exercise price – the price at which, if the option is exercised, the option holder will pay to buy (in the case of a call) or receive from a sale of (in the case of a put) the underlying stock or other instrument in the quantity specified in the contract.

Risk-free rate of return – necessary to value the option because those granting the option (known as "option writers") must, in theory, finance a purchase of the underlying stock to deliver at the exercise price (in the case of a call option) or have the cash available to buy the underlying stock at the exercise price (in the case of a put option). The risk-free rate of return is therefore a proxy for what this will cost and must therefore be incorporated in the options price.

Volatility of underlying – a crucial variable. We explored the nature of volatility more thoroughly in Magic Number 15. The reason for its importance is that high levels of volatility make exercise more likely, and low levels make it less likely. It must therefore be factored into the market price of the option.

Time to expiry/expiry date – the remaining life of the option is important, because the time value of the options decays progressively more rapidly as expiry approaches. All options expire on known future dates.

WHERE'S THE DATA?

Price of underlying – in a financial newspaper or website.

Type of option – set by the terms of the option contract. You can specify whether you buy a call or a put.

Exercise style – specified in the terms of the option contract. In practice, options on stocks are usually American-style; options on indexes can be either American- or European-style. You, as the buyer, can choose.

Exercise price – stated in the terms of the option contract. You can choose from a range of exercise prices.

Risk-free rate of return – the usual central bank minimum lending rate available from a central bank website or a financial newspaper or website.

Volatility of underlying – can be calculated from first principles, as described in Magic Number 15. What is more normal, however, is that option-pricing models are used to calculate the volatility implied by a given option price. This is because the market price of the option is generally known and obtainable from options-exchange websites or the financial press. Most option-pricing models allow the user the choice of either calculating an option's price from a given level of volatility or an option's implied volatility from a given price.

Time to expiry/expiry date – all options expire on known future dates, set by the options exchange where they are listed. Details of these dates are available from the option exchange's website. Some options expire monthly, but most expire on the basis of a quarterly cycle. Most option-valuation models require you to submit the time to expiry in the form of the number of days. Hence, we need to calculate the number of days from dates, much as we did for the accrued-interest calculation in Magic Number 3.

Calculating it – the Theory

The screenshot in Figure 19.1 shows the delta value (highlighted) for a Venusbank American-style call option with a strike price of 50, and underlying price of 75 and with 100 days to go to expiry, a risk-free market interest rate of 2.25% and volatility of 38%.

Figure 19.1 Calculating the "Magic Number" for . . . Delta and Gamma

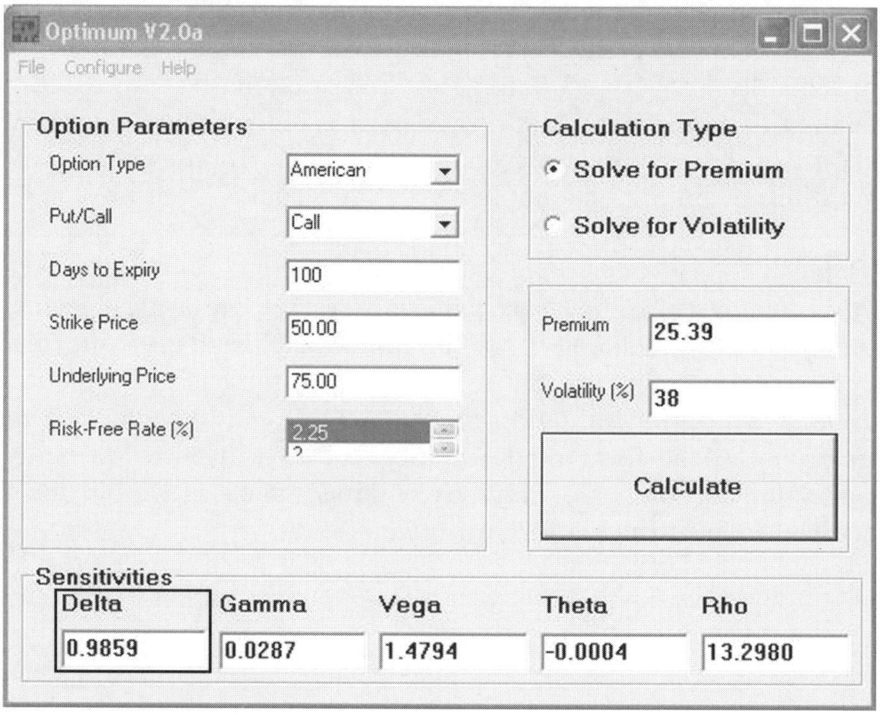

© Nigel Webb Software

The delta value of 0.9859 suggests that for every one penny or one cent movement in the price of the underlying, the value of the option will rise by 0.9859 pence or cents. Gamma is 0.0287.

CALCULATING IT FOR
S&P 500 JULY 1200 PUTS

Figure 19.2 Calculating Delta and Gamma for the S&P 500 July 1200 Puts

Let's now look at how this works with a real-life option. As an example, we are using the July S&P 1200 Put. It is currently 4th June and the option expires on 17th July, making 43 days to go to expiry. The price of the option is 83, volatility 16.4%, the strike price 1,200, the current value of the underlying index 1,116.64, and we assume the risk-free rate of interest to be 2.75%. The screenshot shows the "Greeks" for this option.

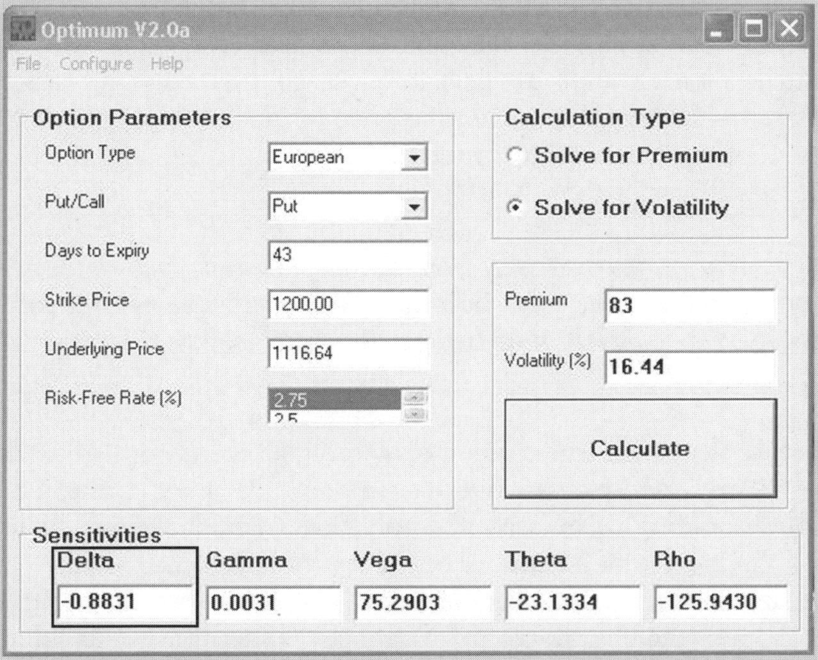

© Nigel Webb Software

The delta value is −0.8831, which means that for every one-point change in the index, the put option's value moves in the opposite direction by 0.8831 points. The gamma value shows that, for example, were the index value to move up by a point to 1117.64, that is the degree of the put option's "in the money-ness" is decreasing, the delta would fall from −0.8831 to −0.8800.

What They Mean

Delta and gamma are useful concepts, because they allow us to work out an approximation for the profit potential of an option purchase, or at least one that assumes a given movement in the underlying shares or index. If we are using options to hedge, the delta allows us to calculate how many put option contracts to buy, for example, to hedge a long position in the underlying.

If, for example, you own 10,000 shares in Venusbank, and the put option delta is –0.9, you would need 11.1 × standard 1,000-share put option contracts to provide a perfect hedge. Buying the 10 contracts that you might think would represent your underlying 10,000-share holding won't provide the precise hedge you want. Buying 11 contracts rather than 10 gets as close to perfection as makes no difference. It means that were the price of the underlying to fall, your profit on the option contracts would almost exactly offset your unrealized loss in the underlying.

There may be reasons why you want to do this sort of thing. You may not want to sell your holding and crystallize a capital-gains tax liability, especially if you believe the price setback is likely to be temporary.

The problem with this technique, of course, is that option contracts are "lumpy" and private investors in particular may not have a large enough holding to be able to apply this "delta hedging" technique with any degree of accuracy. In theory, too, you may need to adjust the size of your hedge over the life of the trade to reflect changes in the delta as the underlying price changes. This is known as "dynamic hedging" and is widely used by professionals. Private investors rarely have holdings large enough to make the technique worthwhile.

The same hedging techniques can be applied to covered warrants (see Magic Numbers 24 and 25). Warrants are a somewhat more flexible tool in this respect because you can deal in warrants in exact numbers of underlying shares rather than pre-set contract sizes.

As we have stressed before, it is worth keeping in mind that option terminology and the concepts described in this and other sections relating to options, are universally applicable in whatever market you happen to use. The only items likely to change are those set by the exchanges themselves. These include contract sizes and expiry dates. In most other respects, what is good for an option trader in the UK or the US applies equally well in Australia, Hong Kong, Japan or Singapore.

MAGIC NUMBER 20

Vega, Rho and Theta

THE DEFINITION

In Magic Number 19 we looked at delta and gamma, two of the five most commonly used "Greeks" – variables denoted by Greek letters that enable you to analyze an option in more detail. The others are *vega*, *rho* and *theta*.

They can be simply described as follows:

vega (the Greek "V", for volatility) is the sensitivity of the option's price to a specific change (normally a one-percentage-point change) in volatility.

rho (the Greek "R", for rate) is the sensitivity of the option price to a specific change in the rate of interest assumed in the option-pricing model.

theta (the Greek "T", for time) is the sensitivity of the option's price to the passage of time, normally the elapsing of one day.

THE FORMULA

In shorthand terms, using an italic "*d*" thus to indicate change, the formulas are as follows:

vega = dOP/dV

rho = dOP/dR

theta = dOP/dT

In these formulas, OP means "option price", and V, R and T signify volatility, interest rate and time, respectively.

Needless to say, the full formulas are much more complex than this, but since these parameters are commonly calculated in all decent option-pricing models, we are going to focus below on how to interpret them.

The Components

The components are those required to be entered into an option-pricing model to establish the fair value of an option, as shown in Magic Numbers 17 and 19. In looking at these three variables, however, we are particularly focusing on:

Rate of interest assumed – the rate of interest affects the option's price because those granting the option (known as "option writers") must in theory finance a purchase of the underlying stock to deliver at the exercise price (in the case of a call option) or have the cash available to buy the underlying stock at the exercise price (in the case of a put option). Hence, option prices are sensitive to changes in the cost of funds. Higher rates of interest mean higher option prices, other things being equal.

Volatility of underlying – volatility is one of the big influences over option prices. The reason for its importance is that high levels of volatility make exercise more likely, and low levels make it less likely. It must, therefore, be factored into the market price of the option.

Time to expiry/expiry date – the remaining life of the option, normally calculated in terms of the number of days to expiry, affects an option's price because the time value of the option decays progressively more rapidly as expiry approaches. All common options expire on known future dates.

Where's the Data?

Rate of interest assumed – the convention is to use a risk-free rate of return, such as the usual central bank minimum lending rate available from a central bank website or a financial newspaper or website or the redemption yield on a short-dated government bond. Some traders use the rate for the time period that corresponds to the remaining life of the option – the rate for three-month money for an option that has three months to run, the six-month rate for an option that has six months to run, and so on. Others might use the rate at which they can borrow.

Volatility of underlying – you can calculate this from first principles, as described in Magic Number 15. What is more usual, however, is that option-pricing models are used to calculate the volatility implied by a given option price, since the market price of the option is generally known and obtainable from options-exchange websites or the financial press. Most option-pricing models allow the user the choice of either calculating an option's price for a given level of volatility or an option's implied volatility for a given price.

Time to expiry/expiry date – all options expire on known future dates, set by the options exchange where they are listed. Details of these dates are available from the option exchange's website. Some options expire monthly, but most expire on the basis of a quarterly cycle. Most option-valuation models require you to submit the time to expiry in the form of number of days. Hence, we need to calculate the number of days from dates, much as we did for the accrued-interest calculation in Magic Number 3.

CALCULATING IT – THE THEORY

The screenshot in Figure 20.1 shows how a standard option-pricing model produces the highlighted "Greeks". For simplicity, we use the same parameters as shown in Figure 19.1.

VEGA, RHO AND THETA   141

Figure 20.1   Calculating the "Magic Number" for ... Vega, Rho and Theta

This is an American-style call option with a strike price of 50, an underlying price of 75, 100 days to go to expiry, a risk-free market interest rate of 2.25% and volatility of 38%. The "Greeks" are: vega 1.4794; theta –0.0004; rho 13.298. The option's price, or premium, is 25.39.

Theta is negative because an option's price inevitably falls as time elapses, all other things being equal.

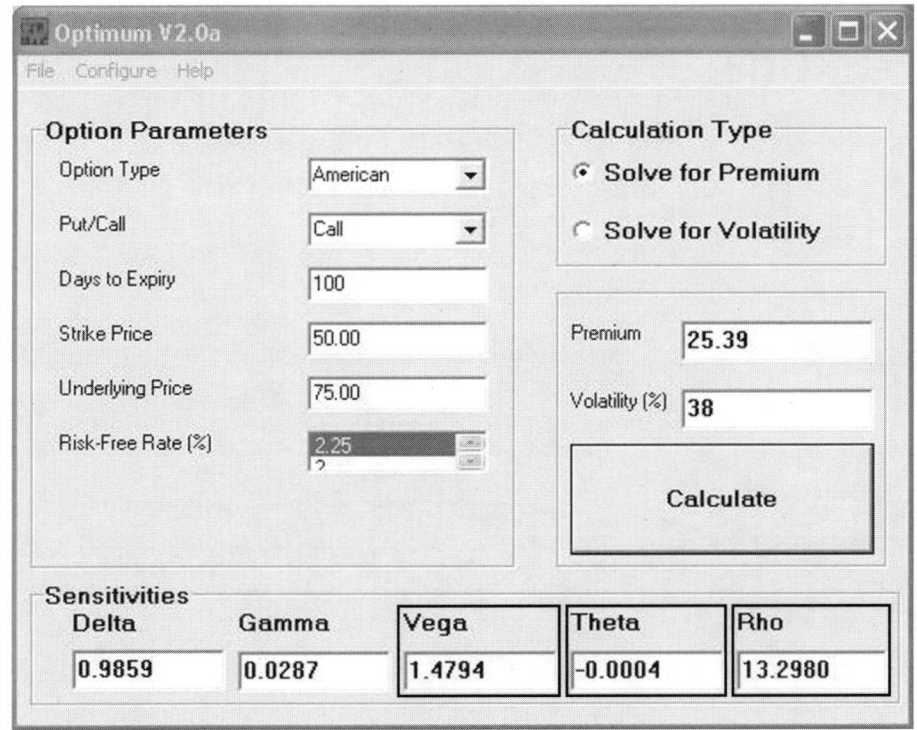

© Nigel Webb Software

We need to take care interpreting these numbers too literally. For instance, in this example a rho of 13.298 does not mean that the price of the option rises by 13.3 points from 25 to 38 if interest rates go up by one percentage point. In fact, the movement in this event is from 25.39 to 25.52; in other words, by 13.298 divided by 100. The same is also true of vega, where a one-point change in volatility affects the option price by 0.014794. The impact of theta in this instance is negligible. This variable comes into its own for short-dated options (say, for example, those with less than 30 days to expiry), where time value erodes progressively more quickly.

CALCULATING IT FOR
S&P JULY 1200 PUT

Figure 20.2 Calculating "The Greeks" for the S&P July 1200 Put (I)

Option Parameters	**Calculation Type**
Option Type: European	● Solve for Premium
Put/Call: Put	○ Solve for Volatility
Days to Expiry: 43	
Strike Price: 1200.00	Premium: 85.86
Underlying Price: 1116.64	Volatility (%): 17.30
Risk-Free Rate (%): 1 / 0.75	Calculate

Sensitivities

Delta	Gamma	Vega	Theta	Rho
-0.8776	0.0031	77.7531	-46.4317	-125.5613

© Nigel Webb Software

Here, we are using a similar option to the one we used to illustrate delta and gamma in Magic Number 19. This is the S&P July 1200 Put. It is currently 4th June and the option expires on 17th July, making 43 days to go to expiry. The price of the option is 85, volatility 17.3%, the strike price 1,200, the current value of the underlying index 1,116.64, and we assume the risk-free rate of interest is 1%. The screenshot shows the "Greeks" for this option.

As we can see, the values are: vega 77.75; theta –46.43; rho –125.56. Once again, we need to divide by 100 to get to the impact of a one-point change in the underlying variable – a percentage point in the case of vega and rho, and a one-day change in the case of theta.

What it Means

The important point here is that these sensitivities demonstrate how a range of conflicting variables – some positive, some negative – can affect the price of an option. The passage of time has a negative impact on option prices. Falling rates and higher volatility have a positive effect: higher rates and falling volatility have a negative effect. This is over and above the change in the option price caused by a movement in the underlying security or index, as measured by the option's delta.

The upshot is that you can make assumptions about how an option's price will behave if certain events come to pass, and then alter the assumptions to see how the price of the option, and therefore the profitability of the trade, might be affected.

You might, for instance, base a trade on the assumption that the S&P 500 will fall to 1,000 in three weeks' time and that volatility will rise to 25%, and rates will remain unchanged. Figure 20.3 shows how, by plugging this into the pricing model we used in Figure 20.2, the option price in this eventuality would rise from 85 to 199, even though the option now has only 22 days left to expiry.

MAGIC NUMBERS FOR BONDS AND DERIVATIVES

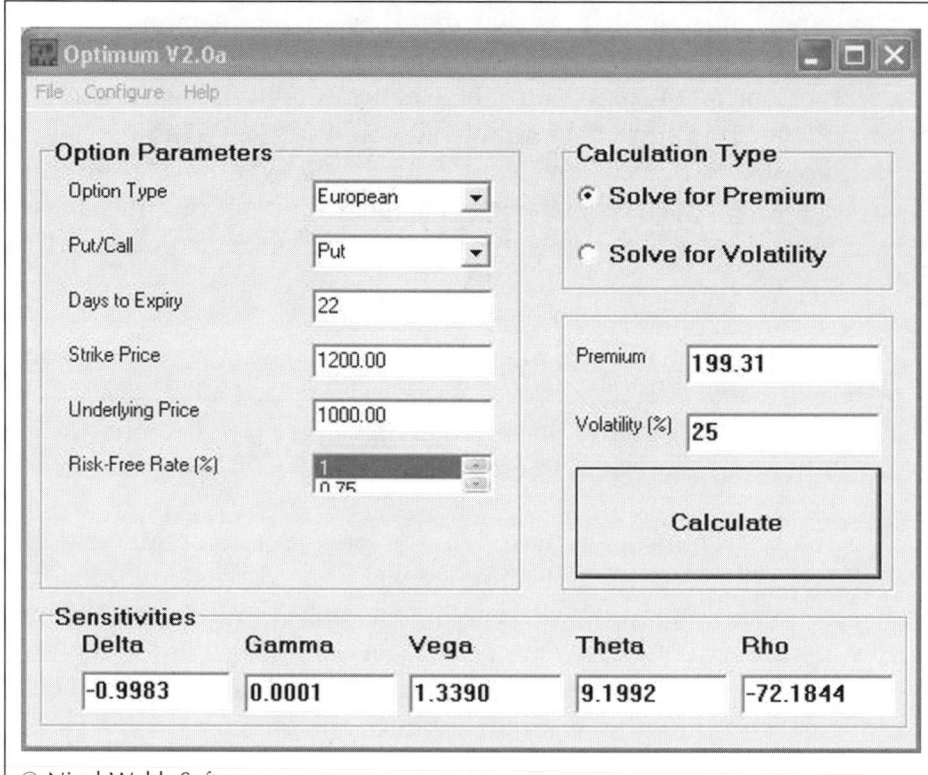

Figure 20.3 Calculating "the Greeks" for the S&P July 1200 Put (II)

© Nigel Webb Software

Note that the value of all the "Greeks" has changed too. It is by using option valuation models in this way and by integrating them with market price predictions arrived at using their techniques, such as technique analysis of price charts, that traders assess while option trades are likely to prove the most profitable.

MAG1C NUM8ER 21 Returns on Covered Call Writing

THE DEFINITION

"Writing a covered call" occurs where the holder of a parcel of shares sells (or "writes") a call option in that stock that is "covered" by his or her shareholding. In other words, if the buyer of the option exercises it, the stock can be delivered from the option writer's own shareholding.

This is a common procedure and is used as a way for holders to generate additional income from their portfolio. It works especially well if you believe the market is likely to be fairly stable over the life of the option. The income generation derives from the fact that an option writer gets the premium (i.e. price) the option buyer pays to acquire the option. The premium is the reward for the writer of the call option assuming the obligation to deliver the underlying stock at the exercise price if called to do so.

In practice, all the would-be "writer" of the option does is sell an appropriate out-of-the-money call option in the market. An out-of-the-money call option is one where the current price of the underlying share is below the exercise price of the option. In other words, the shares have to rise significantly for it to be worthwhile for the option holder to exercise the option.

The maximum number of option contracts that can be sold (or "written") by the option writer is a number whose underlying shares would not exceed his or her holding. If options are based on 1,000-share blocks of the underlying shares – as they are in the UK, for example – and a holder has 3,000 shares, then the maximum number of contracts that can be written in "covered" form in that particular stock is three.

The returns on covered calls cater for the two positive outcomes that can result from a trade like this. They are known as the "static return" and the "if-called return".

The static return assumes that the price of the underlying shares always stays somewhere between the current price and the (higher) exercise price during the life of the option.

In this eventuality, the writer keeps the underlying stock and receives the option premium plus any dividends paid on the underlying shares in the meantime. This is the top half of the fraction.

The bottom half of the fraction is the price of the underlying shares at the time the trade is executed minus the income received from the option premium.

The fraction is expressed as a decimal and then annualized, since the life of the option will almost certainly be less than a year. The correct way to annualize a return is to divide the days to expiry into 365 and then to raise 1 plus the return (in decimal format) to that power, and subtract 1 from the result and convert the resulting number back to a percentage.

The if-called return assumes the option is exercised against the writer, who must then sell the stock at the exercise price to the option holder. In this case, the return is the difference between the current price and the exercise price, plus the option premium, plus any dividend received prior to exercise.

The bottom half of the fraction, as before, is the value of the underlying shares at the time the trade is placed minus the income received from the option premium.

The fraction is expressed as a decimal and then annualized, since the life of the option will almost certainly be less than a year. The correct way to annualize a return is to divide the days to *exercise* into 365 and then to raise 1 plus the return to that power, and subtract 1 from the result and then multiply by 100 to reconvert the result to a percentage.

The examples make it clear how this works.

The Formulas

$SR = (OP + D) \times 100/(UP - OP)$

$ICR = ((EP - UP) + (OP + D)) \times 100 / (UP - OP)$

Where ...

OP = option premium

D = dividend paid (if any)

UP = underlying price

EP = exercise price

Annualization is performed as follows:

$AR = ((1 + R)^{Pwr} - 1) \times 100\%$

Where $Pwr = 365/(DE - DT)$ and

R is the percentage return expressed as a decimal

DT = day of trade

DE = day of expiry or exercise, whichever happens first.

The Components

Option premium — another name for the price of the option itself. As the writer, you receive the premium when you initiate the trade, and keep it under all circumstances. This is your reward for assuming the obligation to deliver stock to the option holder at the exercise price if called to do so during the life of the option.

Dividend — since you are only granting an option over shares you own, and not selling them outright, you keep any dividends that might be paid prior to the exercise of the option, or its expiry, whichever happens first.

Underlying price — the price of the underlying shares on the day you initiate the trade by writing the option.

Exercise price — the price you receive for the shares underlying the option contract if the writer exercises the option before expiry. Options are issued with a range of expiry dates and exercise prices. Covered calls invariably start out as out-of-the-money options, which means that the exercise price is higher than the underlying prices of the shares at the outset.

Day of trade — the day you initiate the trade.

Day of expiry or exercise — in the case of most options used in this particular technique, exercise can take place any time prior to expiry, although it will only happen if it is in the option holder's financial interest to do so. All options have pre-set expiry dates that are known in advance.

WHERE'S THE DATA?

Option premium – the price you receive from the sale of the option. Current prices can be found from the website of the exchange in question (for example, www.liffe.com in the case of the UK options market). The price you receive is the bid price of the option you choose. Beware of relying on newspapers for option prices, since they only quote middle-market prices and the bid price may be significantly less.

Dividend – the timing of pending dividend payments can be checked by calling up the company secretary, from a statistical service, or from the financial calendar in the company's latest annual report or interim statement.

Underlying price: can be found from a financial newspaper or from a financial website.

Exercise price – you choose the option with the most advantageous exercise price; that is, the one that potentially gives the best return with the least risk of exercise. This requires exercising judgment. Exercise prices occur at pre-determined price intervals that are usually round numbers. The range of possible exercise prices can be found from the exchange's website. Daily financial papers usually give only details of a small number of the available options.

Day of trade – this is self-evident.

Day of expiry or exercise – the exercise date is only known after the event. The expiry date for the option can be found from the option exchange's website. Options on different stocks often have different expiry months, although the day of the month is usually based on a particular convention, such as, for example, the third Thursday of the month in question. The "days to expiry" or "days to exercise" can then be calculated using a diary or days-from-dates table.

Calculating it – the Theory

Figure 21.1 shows the different numbers to be pulled from the sources described and how to use them to calculate the ratio.

Figure 21.1 Calculating the "Magic Number" for ... Static and "If-called" Returns

You are planning to write a covered call in the Planet of Jupiter Enterprises August 550 option series. The current price is 520p, the option premium is 10p, no dividend is payable before expiry, today's date is 3rd June (day 154) and the option expires on 17th August (day 229).

Static return

Static return is.. 1.96%
(working) $(10 \times 100/520 - 10)$

Annualization factor is... 4.8666
(working) $(365/(229 - 154))$

Annualized static return is.. 9.91%
(working) $((1.0196^{4.8666}) - 1.00) \times 100$

If-called return

Assume the option is exercised by the holder on 1st August (day 213), in 59 days' time.

If-called return is... 7.80%
(working) $(10 + (550 - 520)) \times 100/(520 - 10)$

Annualization factor is... 6.19
(working) $(365/(213 - 154))$

Annualized if-called return is 59.19%
(working) $((1.078^{6.19}) - 1.00) \times 100$

On an annualized basis, the return is highly attractive.

CALCULATING IT FOR
MARKS & SPENCER

Figure 21.2 Calculating the Returns for ... Writing the Marks & Spencer September 390 Calls

The figures ...

Trade date	3rd June, 2004 (day 155)
Expiry date	17th September, 2004 (day 261)
Exercise price	390p
Underlying price	366p
Option premium	10.75p
Dividend	Final dividend of 7.1p payable on 16th July

The calculations ...

Static return

Static return is 5.02%
(working) $(10.75 + 7.1) \times 100/(366 - 10.75)$

Annualization factor is 3.443
(working) $365/(261 - 155)$

Expiry is on day 261 and trade day is day 155. There are 106 days to expiry. To calculate the annualized return we raise 1.00 plus the return calculated above expressed as a decimal to the power 3.443 and then subtract 1.00 from the result

Annualized static return is 18.31%
(working) $((1.0502^{3.443}) - 1.00) \times 100$

If-called return

Assume the option is exercised by the holder on 1st August (day 214), in 59 days' time.

If-called return is 11.78%
(working) $(7.1 + 10.75 + (390 - 366)) \times 100/(366 - 10.75)$

or .... (4,185.00/355.25)

Annualization factor is 6.19
(working) $365/(214 - 155)$

Annualized if-called return is 99.24%
(working) $((1.1178^{6.19}) - 1.00) \times 100$

What it Means

Writing covered calls is often described as one of the best-kept secrets in the market. It is hard to think of a downside to them.

Look at the alternative scenarios:

Stock that is called away is sold at a higher price than would otherwise have been earned (after taking the option premium into account).

If the option expires unexercised, additional portfolio income has been generated.

If the underlying stock falls in price, then the option premium received provides a little cushion, and if necessary, rather than be locked into a falling stock, the holder can unwind the trade by buying back the option and selling the underlying.

This technique relies on making a judgment about the likely price volatility of the underlying stock. The ideal time to put on trades like this is when volatility is relatively high but looks like falling, because this is the time when option prices will be at their highest.

The big problem is that some option brokers find this administratively burdensome. Uncovered writing of options is considered to be very risky indeed and not recommended for the average investor, which means that a broker needs to have the comfort of knowing that the underlying shares are held by the client, in order to cover the eventuality of an option exercise.

Many brokers get round the problem by simply banning clients from writing options under any circumstances. So, if this technique appeals to you but your broker adopts such an approach, you may need to find a new broker.

Finally, beware of placing too much reliance on annualized returns. They are best used to compare the relative merits of different choices of covered-call writing propositions.

This is because the drawback to the annualization process is that it assumes that the option trade that gave rise to the initial return can be replicated in quick succession throughout the year, which is unlikely to be the case. Even so, returns generated by these trades are often attractive in their own right.

MAGIC NUMBER 22

The Put–Call Ratio

THE DEFINITION

The put–call ratio is the volume of put options traded in a particular underlying security or index divided by the volume of call options in it. The underlying in question can be a stock, an index or a commodity. Alternatively, the volume of all index and equity options traded on a particular exchange can be used as the basis, to get a value for the market as a whole. The ratio is used as a way of gauging market sentiment. Graphing the ratio over a period of days may provide some perspective.

THE FORMULA

PCR = put volume (in numbers of contracts)/
      call volume (in numbers of contracts)

THE COMPONENTS

Put-option volume – the trading volume in all put options for the underlying security or index, expressed in numbers of contracts.

Call-option volume – the trading volume in all call options for the underlying security or index, expressed in numbers of contracts.

WHERE'S THE DATA?

Put- and call-option volume – derivatives exchanges publish this data on a daily and monthly basis and some of this information is published in the financial press. It is important, however, to distinguish trading volume data from open interest (the number of contracts carried on from one trading day to the next). This should not be used in the ratio.

In general, the ratio is used to gauge broad market sentiment; so the more all-encompassing the data, the better.

Calculating it — the Theory

Figure 22.1 shows the different numbers to be pulled from the sources described and how to use them to calculate the ratio.

Figure 22.1   Calculating the "Magic Number" for ... Put–Call Ratio

The Uranus stock exchange trades equity and index options.
The USE Gazette gives the following data for option volume.

	Puts (no. of contracts)	Calls (no. of contracts)
USE500 Index	16,005	10,751
Equity options	26,444	24,759
Total	42,449	35,510

The put–call ratio for the index is 1.49
(working) (16,005/10,751)

The put–call ratio for the market is 1.20
(working) (42,449/35,510)

These numbers differ somewhat, although the general impression is of a market that is mildly bearish. The values cannot be called extreme, and therefore there is no case for adopting a contrarian view.

> ### CALCULATING IT FOR
> # MAJOR MARKET INDICES
>
> **Figure 22.2 Calculating the Put–Call Ratio for Some Major Market Indices**
>
> **The figures ...**
>
> On 2nd June, 2004, the volume of put and call options in certain major market indices was as follows:
>
> | | Puts (contracts) | Calls (contracts) |
> |---|---|---|
> | S&P500 | 32,836 | 22,789 |
> | FTSE100 | 74,757 | 46,746 |
> | DAX | 298,664 | 525,075 |
>
> **The put–call ratios for the respective indices are:**
>
> **S&P500** **1.44**
> (working)   (32,836/22,789)
>
> **FTSE100** **1.60**
> (working)   (74,757/46,746)
>
> **DAX** **0.57**
> (working)   (298,664/525,075)
>
> Note that a ratio of less than 1.0 indicates positive market sentiment (more calls than puts traded). The absolute level of contract numbers is irrelevant, because of differences in contract value and definition between exchanges.

WHAT IT MEANS

The value of this ratio as a predictive tool rests on two principles. One is that options are widely used for speculating on directional movements in the market. The second is that it is widely followed by short-term market analysts and hence can to some degree become a self-fulfilling prophecy.

However, interpreting put–call ratios is something of an art. It is, for example, clear that the higher the ratio, the more bearish sentiment is becoming. The more puts are traded, the more worried investors are about the stock or stock index and are therefore seeking to speculate on a fall or insure against it.

You can calculate the ratio, as we implied earlier, for individual stocks. The drawback to this is that the data can be confused by events (for instance, company results) that are specific to that stock and less of a pointer for the market as a whole.

Most traders, therefore, confine their study of the put–call ratio to the options on a widely traded stock market index such as the S&P 500, the FTSE 100 or the Nikkei 225. This gives a broad view of market sentiment.

It gets more complicated, however. While you can read the data strictly at face value, if the measurements get extreme – in other words, the put–call ratio spikes – then it is sometimes used as a contrary indicator. A sharp upward spike in the ratio, indicating a climate of fear in the stock market, may be construed as a signal that it's right to buy, at least on a short-term basis. This is because it is often profitable to buy in moments of panic. Prices invariably revert to some sort of mean, allowing a nimble trader to profit. The key here is that the spike has to be an extreme one.

By the same token, if optimism is such that the put–call ratio is hitting new lows (many more calls being bought than puts), then the chances are, as this gets to the extreme stage, that the market is riding for a fall. Selling at times of market euphoria is usually a good thing, as those rare investors who sold technology stocks in March 2000 will bear out.

The big question is, when does normal bearishness or bullishness turn into panic selling or buying, and change into a sign that astute investors should do the opposite to the crowd? There is no precise way of gauging this, and it is perhaps best to look for other signals to confirm the prevailing mood.

Part Four

Convertibles and Warrants "Magic Numbers"

Convertibles and Warrants "Magic Numbers"

In this final part of the book, we continue our look at some of the basic parameters we need to understand to use other derivatives, and bonds that incorporate options.

In Magic Numbers 24 and 25, we look at warrants. These are similar to options, but with their own tools, analysis techniques and peculiarities. In Magic Number 23, which deals with convertible bonds, the instrument in question is a hybrid of a bond and an option. It also has its specific analytical ratios.

For a convertible bond, the key ratios are *conversion premium* and *payback period*. The conversion premium compares the effective price at which the conversion can take place – which is a function of the conversion terms and the price of the bond – with the current share price.

The payback period compares the income differential between the bonds and the shares to work out how long it would take a conversion of the bond into equity to pay back the premium for converting it.

Traditional warrants are typically long-expiry, out-of-the-money, European-style call options. There are two common ways of valuing these for comparative purposes: the *breakeven rate* and the *capital fulcrum point*. The breakeven rate calculates the annual percentage growth rate in the underlying equity required to leave the warrant exactly at the breakeven point (of exercise price plus premium paid) at expiry.

The capital fulcrum point calculates the growth required in the underlying shares to leave the performance of the shares and the warrants identical.

Magic Number 25 looks at some other ratios related to "covered" warrants. This new market is becoming increasingly popular. Essentially, covered warrants are options, but with terms that are not standardized by an exchange. They typically have longer expiries and are less "lumpy" in terms of the contract size. They cannot be "written" by investors as options can.

The "cover" concept in covered warrants refers to the number of warrants that need to be bought to equate to one share of the underlying. You can substitute covered warrants in the formulas for breakeven rate and capital fulcrum point by substituting the covered warrant price multiplied by cover ratio for the traditional warrant price in the formula.

The covered warrant "magic numbers" we look at here are *gearing* and *elasticity*, which essentially show the way that the warrant price responds to a change in the price of the underlying. Understanding covered warrants draws on knowledge of the ratios used to assess options, so make sure you have read the options sections (Magic Numbers 17–21 and Magic Number 15) before you tackle the last part of the book.

As in the previous three parts of this book, we think that all of these "magic numbers" are absolutely basic to informed investing using convertibles and warrants, whether traditional or covered. They are all used by the professionals, but are relatively easy to calculate with a simple understanding of algebra, a financial calculator or spreadsheet program, and a computerized option or warrant valuation model.

The sections that follow examine each of these three "magic number" groups in more detail. Read on to find out how to get the data you need, how to calculate them and what they mean.

Magic Number 23: Convertible Bonds – Conversion Premium and Payback

The Definition

Convertible bonds allow a holder to convert the bond into shares of the issuer under certain circumstances. Typically, the conversion period will only begin some time after the bond is issued and at an effective price higher than the share price at the time the bond is issued. There may be conditions attached to the convertible, such as the share price remaining a significant amount above the conversion price for several weeks.

In effect, a convertible is a conventional bond with an out-of-the-money call option attached. Hence, it is a hybrid of bond and option. In theory, both components can be valued separately.

From the standpoint of most convertible-bond buyers, however, a different method is employed to value the convertible. This looks at the implied price of the share as defined by the terms of the convertible, disregarding whether or not it is worth exercising the conversion right immediately. The resulting theoretical conversion price of the bond is then compared with the current share price. It will normally be higher, because otherwise conversion would have taken place already. How much higher is called the "conversion premium".

Convertible bonds usually offer a higher yield than the underlying share into which they are convertible. The payback period measures how long it would take for this favourable income advantage to eliminate the conversion premium.

The Formula

Market conversion price = price of convertible bond/conversion ratio

Income differential = (coupon − (conversion ratio × dividend))/conversion ratio

Conversion premium = (MCP − SP) × 100/SP

(where MCP = market conversion price and SP = share price)

Payback period (in years) = (MCP − SP)/income differential.

Note that the conversion premium is calculated in terms of the implied price of the underlying shares rather than the convertible, although both prices are used in the calculation. Calculating conversion premium and payback allows investors to evaluate the merits of a range of convertible bonds, and pick the best. The surest way to get the calculations right is to look at the relevant cash flows to work out the numbers.

The Components

Price of convertible – the market price of the convertible, normally expressed, as most bond prices are, as a percentage of the face value.

Price of underlying shares – the market price of the underlying shares.

Conversion ratio – defines the terms under which conversion takes place. Conversion terms typically specify a period of time or specific future dates when conversion rights can be exercised and the number of shares to which a holder of a fixed nominal amount of the bond is entitled.

Bond coupon – the annual coupon on the convertible bond.

Dividend on the shares – the annual dividend payment on the shares.

Where's the Data?

Price of convertible – often quoted alongside the underlying equity in the share price pages of daily financial newspapers, on bond-related websites, or from the company itself. Some financial sites charge for access to bond data, and bond prices in general are covered less extensively in the financial press than stock prices.

Price of underlying shares – can be found from the price pages of a daily financial newspaper or a financial website.

Conversion ratio – the definitive terms will be found in the listing particulars or an equivalent document (such as an SEC filing) for the bond. It is always worth checking the small print of conversion terms to make sure that there are no extra conditions attached to conversion. Indeed, you may have to hunt in the document to discover the exact conversion terms as well.

Bond coupon – will be explicitly stated, often in the price pages of a daily financial newspaper.

Dividend on the shares – can be obtained from recent news releases, the company annual report, direct from the company secretary, or from a reliable statistical service or financial website.

Calculating it – the Theory

Figure 23.1 shows the different numbers to be pulled from the sources described and how to use them to calculate the ratio.

Figure 23.1 Calculating the "Magic Number" for ... Conversion Premium and Payback Period

Solar Superwidgets has a convertible bond in issue with the following terms:

Coupon 4%
Maturity .... 31st December, 2010
Conversion factor .... 2 ordinary shares per bond of $100 nominal
Price of convertible $170
Price of ordinary $70
Annual dividend on ordinary $1.50

In order to work out the ratios, we need to work out the market conversion price and the income differential So, in cash terms,

Market conversion price is $85
(working)   (170/2)

An investor would pay $170 for a $100 nominal bond with the right to subscribe to two shares.

Conversion premium is therefore 21.43%
(working)   ((85 − 70)/70) × 100

That is, the percentage by which the price implied by the convertible's price and the conversion terms exceeds the current price of the shares.

Income differential per $100 bond is equivalent to the difference between the annual coupon on the bond and the annual dividend on two shares.

Income differential is $1
(working)   (4 − (2 × 1.50))

On a per-share basis this needs to be divided by the conversion ratio.

Income differential per share is: $0.50
(working)   ($1/2)
Payback period is .... 30 years
(working)   (85 − 70)/0.5

In per-share terms a holder of the bond recoups $0.50 a year from the better income on the bond but it would take 30 years, other things being equal, for this to erode the $15 gap between the theoretical conversion price implied by the bond and the current value of the shares.

Figure 23.2 is a good example of a recently issued convertible and demonstrates quite well how the calculations work.

CALCULATING IT FOR
SAKS

Figure 23.2 Calculating Conversion Premium and Payback Period for the Saks Inc. 2% Convertible 2024

The figures ...

Saks Inc., the upmarket US retail group, recently issued a convertible note with the following terms:

Conversion terms .... 47.221 shares per $1,000 nominal
Redemption date .... 15th March, 2024
Interest payable .... 15th September and 15th March
Coupon 2%
Price of convertible 102.00%
Price of equity $15.09
Dividend on equity $0.00

The calculation ...

Conversion price is $21.60
(working)   (1,020/47.221)

This is 102% of $1,000 (the cost of $1,000 nominal of the note) divided by the conversion ratio

Conversion premium is 43.14%
(working)   ((21.60 − 15.09) × 100)/15.09

Income differential .... $20 on a $1,000 nominal of note

This is straightforward because there is no dividend on the common stock.

Income differential per potential converted share is $0.42363
(working)   (20/47.221)

Payback period is .... 15.37 years
(working)   (21.60 − 15.09)/0.42363

What it Means

Professionals use ratios like this to compare a range of convertibles and to find the most attractive ones. The alternative method of deciding whether a particular convertible is an attractive proposition is to value the "straight" bond component and the implied call option represented by the conversion terms separately. This is a bit more taxing for private investors to do because, as the Saks example shows, convertible terms rarely conform exactly to standard option contracts.

In the Saks case, for example, the stock price has to remain more than 20% above the conversion price continuously for 20 successive trading days for conversion to be permitted. This is different from a standard American-style option, which can be converted at any time up to expiry if it is in the holder's financial interest to do so.

The 20-year potential expiry date on the Saks convertible is also very much at variance with the usual option, which typically might have at most around nine months to run. That is not to say that a professional investor couldn't value an option like this, but it becomes hard for a regular private investor to do the same unless they have in-depth grounding in finance theory and sophisticated software tools at their disposal.

The other difficult aspect of this is precisely how to value the underlying bond component of the convertible. The best way is to take a company with the same credit rating and with an issued "straight" bond of the same maturity and with the same tax treatment for investors and the same currency denomination, and look at its redemption yield. We can then assume the bond component of the convertible would sell on a similar redemption yield, and work back to a price from that using a financial calculator in the way described in Magic Number 5.

Assuming we can do both of these calculations and arrive at a value for each component, we can then add the price of the bond component to the value of the option and compare the result with the market price of the convertible. The more complex its terms, the bigger are the opportunities for the convertible to be mis-priced.

MAGIC NUMBER 24

Breakeven Rate and Capital Fulcrum Point

THE DEFINITION

The measures in this section are those that have generally been used with traditional warrants (as distinct from covered warrants). The main differences between traditional warrants and covered warrants are that traditional warrants are exclusively call warrants, normally European-style exercise (that is, exercisable only on a specific future day) and that the so-called cover ratio is almost always 1:1. One warrant represents one share.

While this differs from the situation for covered warrants, which are the subject of Magic Number 25, these ratios can be adapted with little difficulty for use with covered warrants too.

The breakeven rate (BER) is the annualized growth in underlying asset price between now and expiry that is required to leave the warrant holder at breakeven on expiry. You find this by adding the exercise price to the price paid for the warrant, and then dividing this total by the current price of the underlying, and expressing the result as an average annual rate over the period to expiry. This can be done easily with a financial calculator.

The capital fulcrum point (CFP) presents the calculation in a slightly different way. It is the rate of annual increase required in the underlying price that would produce identical growth in the warrant price. Any annual increase over the capital fulcrum point would mean the warrant was the better investment of the two. You calculate the CFP by taking the exercise price and dividing it by the underlying price minus the warrant price, and then express the result as a percentage annual rate over the period to expiry.

The Formula

$$\text{BER} = \left\{ [(\text{EP} + \text{WP})/UP]^{1/y} - 1 \right\} \times 100$$

$$\text{CFP} = \left\{ [\text{EP}/(UP - WP)]^{1/y} - 1 \right\} \times 100$$

Where...

EP = exercise price

WP = warrant price (or, in the case of covered warrants, WP × cover ratio)

UP = underlying price

Y = years to expiry

These formulas look complex, but they are simply the mathematical expression of the descriptions in the previous section, and simple to work out if completed in stages. The formulas can be adapted for use with covered warrants by substituting the covered warrant price, multiplied by the cover ratio, for the warrant price element in the formula.

The capital fulcrum point only really works properly for call warrants. The BER can be applied to put warrants as well, although in this case the numerator of the fraction within the formula is the exercise price *minus* the warrant price.

The Components

Exercise price – the price at which the warrant can be converted into the underlying share it represents.

Warrant price – the market price of the warrant.

Underlying price – the price of the underlying shares into which the warrant is exercisable.

Years to expiry – the number of years the warrant has to go until it expires.

WHERE'S THE DATA?

Exercise price – inherent in the terms of the warrant.

Warrant price – available from a financial newspaper or a specialist website.

Underlying price – available in the normal way from a financial newspaper or from a financial website.

Years to expiry – inherent in the terms of the warrant. The expiry date should be expressed in years and decimal fractions of a year, using the exact number of years and days from now to the expiry date.

CALCULATING IT – THE THEORY

Figure 24.1 shows the different numbers to be pulled from the sources described and how to use them to calculate the ratio.

> **Figure 24.1 Calculating the "Magic Number" for ... BER and CFP**
>
> Intergalactic Enterprises has issued call warrants with the following terms:
>
> Exercise price $20
> Current price of stock $13
> Expiry date .... 31st December, 2008
> Today's date .... 30th November, 2004
> Warrant price $3
>
> Breakeven rate is found as follows:
>
> Step one: calculate fraction 1.769
> (working) $(20+3)/13$
>
> Step two: calculate period to expiry .... 4.0849 years
> (working)   (Four complete years plus 31/365)
>
> Compound growth rate is that which 14.99%
> equates 1 to 1.769 over this period .... (using financial calculator)
> (working) $(1.769^{1/4.0849} - 1) \times 100$
>
> **BER is 14.99%**
>
> Capital fulcrum point is found in much the same way:
>
> Step one: calculate fraction 2.000
> (working) $(20/(13-3)$
>
> Step two: calculate period to expiry .... 4.0849 years
> (working)   (Four complete years plus 31/365)
>
> Compound growth rate is that which 18.49%
> equates 1 to 2 over this period .... (using financial calculator)
> (working) $(2^{1/4.0849} - 1) \times 100$
>
> **CFP is 18.49%**

What it Means

Typically, traditional warrants have been issued in smaller UK companies and by some investment trusts (such as Fidelity Asian Values in Figure 24.2). They have not been a particularly active market of late. However, these concepts work equally well in other contexts. The capital fulcrum point can be calculated equally well for European-style calls in the covered warrants market, and the breakeven rate can be applied equally to the covered warrant market in both calls and puts.

Calculating it for
FIDELITY ASIAN VALUES

Figure 24.2 Calculating BER and CFP for ... Fidelity Asian Values

Fidelity Asian Values is a UK-listed investment trust investing in Asian companies. It has issued warrants with the terms described below:

The figures ...

Exercise price	100p
Current price of stock	55.25p
Expiry date	31st December, 2006
Today's date	1st July, 2004
Warrant price	4.5p

The calculations ...
Breakeven rate:

Step one: calculate fraction	1.8914
(working)	(100 + 4.5)/55.25
Step two: calculate period to expiry	2.501
(working)	(two complete years plus 183/365)
Compound growth rate is that which	29.02%
equates 1 to 1.8914 over this period	(using financial calculator)
(working)	$(1.8914^{1/2.501} - 1) \times 100$

BER is 29.02%

Capital fulcrum point

Step one: calculate fraction	1.9704
(working)	(100/(55.25 − 4.50)
Step two: calculate period to expiry	2.501
(working)	(two complete years plus 183/365)
Compound growth rate is that which	31.15%
equates 1 to 1.9704 over this period	(using financial calculator)
(working)	$(1.9704^{1/2.501} - 1) \times 100$

CFP is 31.15%

All that covered warrant investors need to do to use the concepts for covered warrants is perform the calculation using the covered warrant price multiplied by the cover ratio and substitute it for the warrant price in the formulas given earlier. There are more covered warrant ratios in the next section, where there is more explanation.

Ratios like this are useful because they force you to examine the rate of growth that you will require in the underlying share price for the warrant to become profitable.

You can then make a judgment about whether this underlying share price growth is a realistic expectation in light of the outlook for the market and the medium-term returns stock market investing typically generates.

Different warrant choices can also then be compared. Traditional warrants, in particular, are not a perfect market, and performing calculations like this can highlight pricing anomalies.

MAG1C NUM8ER 25
Covered Warrant Gearing

THE DEFINITION

Traditional warrants, when issued, are similar to options and are usually long-dated, out-of-the-money, call options. Covered warrants are similar in concept, but available in both calls and puts. They are available in a number of markets, including the UK, Germany, Italy and Japan.

Covered warrants are normally listed on a stock exchange rather than on a derivatives exchange, and can be traded through a normal stockbroker. They are created by investment banks and do not have to conform to the standard fixed exchange conventions relating to contract size, expiry and strike price intervals. Their terms are, however, always known in advance.

For ordinary share investors who want to speculate on a share, or hedge against an adverse movement in an existing holding, covered warrants are more flexible than options, because they are normally traded in units of one share or less.

As we discovered in the previous section, warrants are priced in a very similar way to options. As with options, the important variables are time to expiry, the difference between the strike price and the underlying price, the price volatility of the underlying, and so on. Moreover, the normal "Greeks" can be worked out for warrants in exactly the same way as for options.

The following additional ratios are, however, relevant to evaluating covered warrants.

Parity, sometimes called the "cover ratio", is the number of warrants that equate to a unit of the underlying. Some warrants are issued with a cover ratio of 1:1 or, in the case of most UK stocks, 10:1. This means 10 warrants equal one underlying share. Index warrants, because of their heavier price, often have cover ratios of 100:1.

Gearing (or leverage) relates the price of the shares to the price of the warrant. It is the ratio of the share price to the warrant price multiplied by parity. It shows the number of shares to which exposure can be gained through an equal money investment in the warrant rather than the share.

Elasticity (sometimes called "effective gearing") shows how much the warrant price will move for a 1% change in the underlying. It is calculated as the delta multiplied by the underlying price divided by the warrant price adjusted for the cover ratio.

The Formula

$G = UP / (WP \times P)$

Where:

G = gearing

UP = underlying price

WP = warrant price

P = parity (cover ratio)

Elasticity = $d \times G$

Where:

d = delta

G = gearing

Using these formulas and the information available from the terms of the warrant, its price and the price of the underlying, we can easily calculate these numbers.

The Components

Underlying price – the market price of the underlying security, be it a share or a stock market index

Warrant price – the market price of the warrant, determined by supply and demand in the market and related to the usual variables governing the price of option-like instruments.

Warrant delta – the change in the price of the warrant for a one-unit change in the price of the underlying security.

Parity – the number of warrants required to equate to one unit of the underlying security.

Where's the Data?

Underlying price – from a financial newspaper or financial website.

Warrant price – normally quoted in financial newspapers and on the issuer's website.

Warrant delta – can be found by plugging the terms of the warrant and its current price into a standard option-valuation model.

Parity – inherent in the terms of the warrant and provided by the issuer in a so-called term sheet of the warrant.

Calculating it – the Theory

Figure 25.1 shows the different numbers to be pulled from the sources described and how to use them to calculate the ratios.

MAGIC NUMBERS FOR BONDS AND DERIVATIVES

> **Figure 25.1 Calculating the "Magic Number" for ... Covered Warrant Ratios**
>
> Milky Way Investment Bank has issued covered warrants in Neptune Superwidgets. Its parameters are shown below:
>
> Type .... European call
> Parity .... 1 warrant for 1 share
> Expiry .... 31st December, 2005
> Strike 250
> Underlying price 200
> Warrant price 7
> Today's date .... 2nd January, 2005
>
> Plugging these variables into a standard option-pricing model provides us with a delta value.
>
> Delta .... 0.2553 (or 25.53%)
> Moving on to calculating the ratios ...
>
> **Gearing is** **28.57**
> (working)   (200/(7 × 1))
>
> **Elasticity is** **7.29**
> (working)   0.2553 × 28.57

Calculating it for
HANG SENG CALL WARRANT

Figure 25.2   Calculating Gearing for ... Hang Seng Index 12,000 December 2004 Call Warrant

The figures ...

SG has issued a call warrant on the Hang Seng Index.
Its parameters are shown below:

Type	European call
Parity	100/1
Expiry	30th December, 2004
Strike	12,000
Underlying price	12,344
Warrant price	95.63
Today's date	9th June 2004
Warrant delta	0.58 (from SG's website)

Moving on to calculating the ratios ...

Gearing is	**1.29**
(working)	(12,344/(95.63 × 100))
Elasticity is	**0.7482**
(working)	(0.58 × 1.29)

What it Means

In reality, using these concepts is simply common sense. If 10 warrants are required to equate to one share, multiplying the warrant's price by 10 will convert it, to all intents and purposes, to an option with the same terms.

The cover ratio allows you to work out concepts like time value, intrinsic value, breakeven points and several other price-based option parameters. Simply multiply up by the cover ratio, do the calculation in the normal way, and then divide the result by the cover ratio, if necessary, to get back to the equivalent in the warrant price.

The big advantage of covered warrants is that they offer the opportunity for investors to hedge some of their shareholdings very efficiently. Because they are denominated in small units, private investors can tailor their exposure much more precisely than is the case with option contracts.

The drawback is that an investment bank, and not an exchange, controls the terms of the warrants that are issued. There is no compulsion on an investment bank to issue a warrant that is convenient for you.

You may, for example, wish to hedge exposure to a share and find that there is no appropriate put warrant issued that fits your requirements.

Where covered-warrant markets have started, the typical pattern is for issuers to begin issuing warrants on the market index, and then move on to a range of large-capitalization shares. If you hold small-capitalization stocks, you may find that hedging using covered warrants simply isn't open to you. This is, however, also true of the options market. For the most part, options and warrants are only available on large-capitalization stocks.

Appendix
Finding the Information

This appendix is designed to make it easy to find the information you need to be able to calculate these "magic numbers" for yourself. We look particularly at websites with relevant resources. Most of the sources mentioned are online, but it is worth remembering too that daily financial newspapers also contain basic information on bonds and derivatives.

We have divided this appendix into sections based on the order in which the broad sections on bonds, futures and options, and warrants appear in the book.

Within each section, the information is grouped under headings that indicate the nature of the information provided.

BONDS

Prices

Bloomberg (*www.bloomberg.co.uk*) has bond prices for benchmark government bonds, plus news and commentary on the bond market covering the Americas, Asia/Pacific and Europe.

Interactive Investor (*www.iii.co.uk*) includes UK government bond and selected corporate bond prices in its portfolio section. This is a free service for registered users.

Bondscape (*www.bondscape.net*) was launched in June 2001 and is a free service designed primarily for professional investment advisers. It offers access to information on 400 UK gilts, European government bonds and sterling-, dollar- and Euro-denominated bonds. The many features include closing prices, news and an overview of bonds, plus a more detailed guide in PDF format.

NASD Bondinfo (*www.nasdbondinfo.com*) has basic descriptive information for over 4,000 US corporate bonds. More will be added in the future. The site can be searched by industry, maturity range or credit rating. The daily list section of the site has additions, deletions or changes for corporate bonds. It is also possible to track up to 100 corporate bonds using a "portfolio" feature. Transactions and statistics can be tracked for individual bonds. Lists of closing prices can be downloaded.

The US Bond Market Association (*www.investinginbonds.com*) has prices for US municipal, corporate and treasury bonds. The extensive information on offer includes investor's guides, research and statistics, plus a useful glossary of bond terms.

Governments

The Bank of England (*www.bankofengland.co.uk*) has details of the Bank's monetary policy work, including interest-rate decisions. The site contains all the material relevant to the Bank's monetary responsibilities. There are various statistical releases and publications, together with an interactive database. The Bank's quarterly "Inflation Report" can be purchased online. This includes an assessment of the medium-term inflation prospects and risks and a summary of monetary policy during the quarter.

The UK Debt Management Office (*www.dmo.gov.uk*) has money-market information including a table of interest rates for the UK, US and Eurozone, historic and current data and end-of-day prices. Information relating to UK government bonds (known as gilts) include the amount issued, the type and issue date. An investor's guide to gilts can be downloaded from the site.

HM Treasury (*www.hm-treasury.gov.uk*) has the latest economic indicators and a forecast for the UK economy. The site contains everything you could possibly wish to know about the workings of the UK's finance ministry, as well as all the speeches delivered by Britain's finance minister.

The Bank of Japan (*www.boj.or.jp/en/*) has monetary policy information, both current and dating back to 1997, including a monthly report of recent economic and financial developments and a bi-annual report on currency and monetary control. Bond market statistics include release schedules, bond market yields and long-term time-series data.

Numerous research papers and reports are also available.

The Japanese Ministry of Finance (*www.mof.go.jp/english/*) has a straightforward guide for investors in Japanese government bonds. Other information includes auction announcements, planned bond issuance and a quarterly bond newsletter.

The European Central Bank (*www.ecb.int*) has numerous statistics available, including monetary statistics, MFI (Monetary Financial Institutions) interest-rate statistics, key characteristics of the euro area, the USA and Japan and statistical press releases. Various free publications are also on offer in many European languages, either in PDF or hard-copy versions. Information on past and present interest rates can be accessed from the home page.

The Federal Reserve (*www.federalreserve.gov*), the US central bank, has comprehensive information on US monetary policy, including policy-making, monetary policy reports to Congress, the purchase and sale of US Treasury and Federal agency securities and email notification for monetary policy press releases. Statistics include interest rates and the performance of Treasury securities compared to other investments. Many other publications and reports are also available.

Further information regarding the United States can be found at **The Bureau of the Public Debt** (*www.publicdebt.treas.gov*). The site has current rates for bonds, secondary market rates and dates for upcoming auctions. A useful feature of the site is an easy-to-understand guide to US Treasury securities. This is for new investors and covers all the relevant information.

The site also has several different pricing tools available. To find a bond's current worth, the online calculator includes current interest rates, the next interest payment date, final maturity dates and year-to-date interest earned. The S*avings Bond Wizard* helps with managing a savings bond portfolio, showing current redemption value, earned interest and other information. Other items on the site include bond earnings reports and various tables.

Calculators

This brings us on to bond calculators. There are many that can be downloaded, in addition to stand-alone physical and web-based financial calculators. Most good financial calculators include worksheets to do bond market arithmetic such as calculating yields, compounding and discounting. Those mentioned below are a few other notable sites.

Calculatorweb (*www.calculatorweb.com*) has an easy-to-use calculator to calculate bond prices and yields. Enter the bond's coupon rate and maturity date and it then computes either price or yield.

CompoundIt! (*www.bondsonline.com*) is a rather more sophisticated product. Two versions are available: the Standard ($24.95) or Professional ($30.00). A demo version is available online free of charge.

FinanCenter (*www.financenter.com*) offers 11 different calculators for US municipal and corporate bonds and Treasury securities free of charge. The same calculators can also be found at The Motley Fool (www.fool.com). The site also features a section on the basics of bond investment.

Investopedia (*www.investopedia.com*) has numerous free calculators available, including yields, coupon rates and duration. The site's tutorial on bond basics may be of interest.

Economics

Economics data is important to the bond market, especially the general state of the economy, the level of interest rates, and prospects for inflation. There are several sites that provide grounding.

Dismal Scientist (*www.dismal.com*) has up-to-the-minute economic information and analysis with real-time coverage of over 180 economic indicators, including data, analysis and charts. Other features include a summary of daily economic news, economic analysis of the global economy, US forecasts reports and detailed forecasts for the business outlook for the different regions and markets around the world.

All of this is available on subscription. This varies from $29.95 per month to $495 for two years (at the time of writing) with a 14-day free trial. A free email economic-indicator newsletter is available, with a choice of either a daily or weekly summary. This lists all the indicators released that day, their value and a brief analysis of the release.

Similarly, **IDEA Bond Trader** (*www.intermoney.com*) offers an unbiased, subscription-based service. Features include comprehensive intra-day bond market commentary, bond market strategy for the US, Europe and Asia, economic previews and reviews and global market overviews and outlooks. The price is $39 per month or $399 per year. There is a seven-day free trial.

Lombard Street Research (*www.lombard-st.co.uk*) provides economic forecasts and other insights into the economic scene, primarily in the UK. There are various levels of subscription. The online service includes access to weekly webcasts, email daily notes and a choice of Lombard Street Research publications delivered by email. Other levels provide further services such as hard-copy reports and the opportunity to attend Lombard Street seminars.

Ratings

Credit ratings on bonds provided by rating agencies affect market perceptions about issuers and lead to changes in bond prices. Here are some sites of rating agencies.

Fitch Ratings (*www.fitchratings.com*) is a rating agency based in London and New York, with offices worldwide. Some free information is available once registered but the ratings delivery service is only available on subscription.

Moody's (*www.moodys.com*) is a widely used, well-respected source for credit ratings, research and risk analysis. Ratings and related information can be accessed once registered, with various other services available on subscription.

Standard and Poors (*www.standardandpoor.com*) offers a ratings service aimed at the professional market which evaluates the credit quality and volatility of bond funds.

General (including news)

The online version of ***Business Week*** (*www.businessweek.com*) has a section devoted to bonds, with the latest news and an email newsletter available once registered. The site also has a guide to investing in bonds, and calculators for US bonds courtesy of Financenter.

The Wall Street Journal (*www.wsj.com*) has news on global events, financial markets and personal finance. Online and print versions are available on subscription, with a limited amount of free content available to non-subscribers.

RiskGrades (*www.riskgrades.com*) is designed to help investors understand market risk. The site has historic risk charts and current bond rankings. It is also possible to input generic bond and bond portfolio details for grading and analyze the results against numerous benchmarks. The site is free to use and available in seven languages.

BondsOnline (*www.bondsonline.com*) has bond prices, databases, newsletters and books, basic bond tutorials and much more. Some of the information is available free of charge, with a one-month preview available for some of the other services.

Kauders Portfolio Management (*www.gilt.co.uk*) manages portfolios of government securities for individuals, trusts and pension funds. Free information includes a summary of the safety of gilts and a downloadable guide giving detailed explanations of gilts, how the gilt market operates and the basic criteria for selecting gilts.

Bondtalk (*www.bondtalk.com*) has information and analysis on the US bond market and the economy. Although primarily a subscription site for bond professionals, a good deal of free information is available, including prices for US Treasury, municipal and corporate bonds and a course in bond basics.

Longbond (*www.longbond.com*) has links to charts, prices, online brokers and a calculator, all mainly for the US market.

FUTURES AND OPTIONS

Most of the best information on futures and options is available from the websites of derivatives exchanges, and several of the most prominent are covered in brief below.

There are two additional points of contact for calculators. **Numa** (*www.numa.com*) has a superb range of online calculators covering futures, options and convertibles. Second, **Nigel Webb Software** has the Optimum system, a simple option-pricing model, available for free download (www.warp9.org/nwsoft). This has been used for the screenshots relating to option valuation used throughout this book.

Those looking for information on the US options market need look no further than the site of **The Chicago Board Options Exchange** (*www.cboe.com*), which features an extensive range of educational material varying from online option courses and webcasts to self-guided tutorials and trading tools.

CBOE trades options in equities, indices, interest rates and exchange traded funds. Free market data is available, including the most-active trades, average daily volumes and market statistics. Real-time market quotes are available for a free 14-day trial and for $19.95 per month thereafter.

The Chicago Board of Trade (*www.cbot.com*) has real-time quotes, charts and news for all products traded on the CBOT (agriculture, interest rates, the Dow Jones, and metals) together with daily market commentaries.

The site features an online interactive tutorial, which explains what a futures contract is and how margin works, and describes some basic strategies. The site also has links to two trading simulators to give experience in trading the CBOT mini-sized Dow contract before trading for real. There are numerous articles on the subject dating back to 2000.

The Chicago Mercantile Exchange (*www.cme.com*) trades futures and options on futures contracts. The difference between the CBOT and the CME lies in the products traded. At the CME these include interest rates, stock indices, foreign exchange and commodity futures. Weather futures are also on offer for the fearless.

Free online information covers areas such as the basics of trading futures and options, and finding and selecting a futures broker. *Web Instant Lessons* covers topics such as "what makes the market move" and "how traders use technical and fundamental analysis to determine price direction". Other, more detailed, courses are available, with fees ranging from $49–$150. Market data is only available for a fee.

Euronext.LIFFE (*www.liffeinvestor.com*) provides private investors with all the information necessary to understand trading futures and options contracts trade in Europe. As an integrated source of information on options in the UK it can hardly be bettered. The site has trading examples, information on the potential risks and rewards of options, press releases and trading tools, plus a trading simulation game.

In association with e-learning specialist Tradebasics, LIFFE has a series of free interactive education modules, varying from a basic understanding of futures and options to more detailed information about the more advanced trading techniques.

A 15-minute delayed data service is available free of charge at www.liffe-data.com. This contains prices of individual equity options and index futures and options traded on the Brussels, Paris and London exchanges and links to live prices for universal stock futures. Substantial information on the underlying shares and the CAC40, BEL20 and FTSE 100 indices is also available, and an intra-day charting service gives an idea of movements in the market.

LIFFE has introduced a Private Investor Broker Access Programme, the aim of which is to work closely with brokers through whom investors can access and trade LIFFE's equity futures and options. Links to these brokers, together with details of their individual offerings, are on the site.

The Hong Kong Exchange (*www.hkex.com.hk*) has investor information on stock futures and options, DIJA futures, warrants and HIBOR (Hong Kong Interbank Offered Rate) futures. Free data and statistics are also available. These include a daily market report, weekly quotations and daily and monthly statistics.

The Tokyo International Financial Futures Exchange (*www.tiffe.or.jp*) has data and statistics on all its products traded, including a daily update, daily movements and charts and trading volume. The exchange offers three-month Euroyen futures and options, three-month Euroyen LIBOR futures and US dollar-Japanese yen currency futures.

The education part of the site, which presumably will contain more information for investors, was under construction at the time of writing.

The Osaka Futures Exchange (*www.ose.or.jp*) offers stock index futures and options and equity options for Japanese indices, plus DJIA futures. Information is limited, with the exception of some price data.

WARRANTS

Covered warrants are a developing market, particularly in Europe. It is increasingly well served with information.

The six major issuers of covered warrants are good sources. **Dresdner Kleinwort Wasserstein** (*www.warrants.dresdner.com*) has various pricing tools on offer to calculate gearing, parity ratio and intrinsic value. A useful feature on the site is an online course which guides the investor through the ins and outs of covered warrants in some detail.

SG Warrants (*www.warrants.com*) is a particularly good site, with a good deal of free information on offer and coverage of major covered-warrant country markets. The *At the Money* magazine features new SG warrants issues, market trends, trading tips, warrant prices and a series of educational articles on warrants. It is available either by email or post.

Weekly technical analysis is provided on every stock and index on which SG issues warrants in association with TRADINGcentral. SG also issues a 36-page comprehensive guide to, for example, UK warrants (and presumably offers the same facility in other markets). This covers topics such as warrant-trading theory and tips on selecting the right warrant for specific purposes. Tools available on the site include a warrant calculator, sensitivity analysis and a glossary of warrant theory.

Goldman Sachs' warrants site (*www.gs-warrants.co.uk*) features various tools to help understand and analyze warrant investments. The site also has a downloadable guide containing a variety of information such as pricing and investment strategies

Commerzbank (*www.warrants.commerzbank.com*) has warrant news plus a daily report. An online brochure is available or, alternatively, a printed brochure can be requested. In addition, there is a glossary of terms, frequently asked questions, a newsletter and "The 10 Commandments" of warrant investing. Online tools include a calculator, a scenario analyzer and a hedge tool.

Guides and pricing tools are available at **TradingLab** (*www.tradinglab.co.uk*), and at **JP Morgan** (*www.jpmorganinvestor.com*).

All the sites feature live quotes and best and worst performers, although some live quotes can be confusing when displayed. SG and Commerzbank display prices and warrant terms in a much clearer format than some other sites.

The McHattie Group (*www.tipsheets.co.uk*) has been publishing advisory newsletters on traditional warrants since 1987 and, more recently, has begun doing the same for covered warrants. The site features a Warrants Documents Library where literature can be downloaded, including a sample copy of the Warrants Alert Newsletter.

Questions can be emailed to Andrew McHattie and the answers will be posted on the site. The site also has a daily email service and "seven steps to success in covered warrants". There are warrant calculators and a pricing service offered in collaboration with Commerzbank. In addition to all these online features, "The Warrant Box", a one-stop resource for warrants, can be delivered by post, free of charge. This covers guides from warrant issuers and material from the McHattie Group.

A free data service is to be introduced in the near future which will make it possible to check prices and compare valuation statistics for all London-listed covered warrants. Once this is up and running, it may prove to be more useful for selecting warrants than broker sites because of its probable greater clarity.

Index

30/360   20
30E/360   20

A

accrued interest   4, 14, 18–20, 22–26, 31–35, 52, 53, 56, 87–90
Actual/365   20, 23
Actual/Actual   20, 22, 56
adjusted current yield   25, 27–29
Altria   122, 128
American-style option   116, 117, 131, 168,
annualization   147, 150, 151, 153
annualize a return   146
'arbitrage'   74, 114
Argentine government bonds   66
assumed inflation rate   52, 53
'at the money'   103, 125, 190

B

Bank of England   182
Bank of Japan   183
basis points   36, 63–67, 87
basis   16, 19–23, 26, 29, 35, 36, 43, 53–56, 62–67, 75, 77–80, 85–87, 89, 90, 92, 96, 97, 119, 133, 140, 150, 154, 157, 166
basis-point value   62, 86, 87, 89, 90
binomial model   117
Black-Scholes   116, 117, 132
Bloomberg   64, 98, 181
Bondscape   83, 88, 181
BondsOnline   184, 186
Bondtalk   186
breakeven points   179
breakeven rate   56, 57, 162, 169, 172

break-even rate of inflation   51, 52
Bureau of Public Debt   183
Business Week   186

C

CalculatorWeb   34, 184
call feature   45–48
call provision   44
call schedule   44
callable bonds   48
capital fulcrum point   161, 162, 169, 170, 172, 173
Chicago Board of Trade   187
Chicago Board Options Exchange   122, 187
Chicago Mercantile Exchange   188
'clean' price   22, 24–28, 88
Colorado River Authority   47
Commerzbank   190, 191
commodities   103, 112
compound interest   7–11, 37
CompoundIt!   184
compounding   4, 7–9, 11–13, 17, 31, 41, 57, 184
contrary indicator   157
conversion period   163
conversion terms   161, 164–168
convertible bonds   161, 163, 164
convexity   62, 86, 92–94, 96–99
convexity adjustment   92, 94, 96–98
convexity measure   93, 96, 97, 99
coupon   3, 4, 8–10, 13–18, 20–29, 31–33, 37–42, 45–47, 50–53, 55–57, 61, 62, 64, 65, 68, 75, 77–79, 81–84, 88–90, 94, 96–98, 164–167, 184
cover ratio   162, 169, 170, 173, 176, 179

covered call 104, 145, 146, 148, 150, 152
covered warrants 136, 151, 161, 162, 169, 170, 172, 173, 175, 179, 180, 189–191
CPI 4, 50, 54, 56
credit quality 36, 67, 186
credit ratings 185, 186
currency risk 65, 67
current yield 25, 27–29, 76–78, 81, 84, 85, 89, 90, 94, 96, 97

D

day-count convention 19–23
days to expiry 111, 112, 121, 123, 139, 141, 146, 149, 151
Debt Management Office 21, 69, 182
default 36, 66, 67
Delta 130, 131, 134–136, 138, 142, 143, 151, 176, 177, 179
delta hedging 136
'dirty' price 14, 22–24, 51, 52, 87–90, 99
discount rate 12–14, 16, 31, 42, 79, 81–83
discounting 4, 7, 12–15, 17, 31, 72, 81, 184
Dismal Scientist 185
Dresdner Kleinwort Wasserstein 189
duration 13, 14, 17, 62, 75–90, 92–94, 96–99, 184
dynamic hedging 136

E

effective gearing 176
EIB 5.625% 2032 78, 85
elasticity 151, 162, 176, 179
embedded option 98
erosion of time value 129
euphoria 157
Eurobond 16, 20, 48, 82
Euronext LIFFE 188
European Central Bank 183
European-style option 116–118, 131, 132
ex-dividend period 20, 22–24
exercise price 116–118, 120, 122, 125, 126, 132, 133, 139, 145–149, 151, 161, 169–173

F

face value 3, 8, 18, 19, 21, 28, 31, 38, 157, 164
fair value of a future 103, 110, 113
fair value on an option 103
Federal Reserve 183

Fidelity Asian Values 172, 173
FinanCenter 184, 186
Fitch Ratings 185
FTSE 100 Future 114
future value 7, 12–14
futures contract 105, 110–112, 187, 188

G

gamma 130, 131, 134–136, 138, 142
gearing 129, 151, 162, 175, 176, 179, 189
Goldman Sachs 190
'Greeks' 103, 130, 131, 135, 138, 140–142, 144, 175

H

Hang Seng Index 179
historic volatility 109, 121
HM Treasury 182
Hong Kong Exchange 189
hypothetical change in yield 75–77, 88, 94, 95

I

IDEA Bond Trader 185
if-called return 104, 146, 150, 151
'in the money' 103, 125, 130, 135
income differential 161, 166, 167
index-linked bonds 50, 53, 58
inflation expectations 58, 74, 78
Interactive Investor 181
interest payment dates 19, 34, 35, 56
interest-on-interest 7, 8, 11, 13, 17, 29, 31
Internal Rate of Return (IRR) 50
intrinsic value 103, 125–129, 179, 189
intrinsic value of an option 125
inverse relationship (between a bond's yield and its price) 28
Investopedia 98, 184

J

Japanese Ministry of Finance 183
'Japanese Simple Yield' 25
JGB 1.3% 2014 23

K

Kauders Portfolio Management 186

L

leverage 176
listing particulars 165
Lombard Street Research 185
Longbond 187

M

Macaulay Duration 81, 82, 84, 85
margin 103, 105, 187
market conversion price 164, 166
Marks and Spencer 51
maturity date 14, 22, 23, 26–29, 32, 34, 35, 38, 42, 44–47, 61–65, 68, 69, 75, 85, 90, 97, 184
McHattie Group 190, 191
modified duration 75–77, 81–85, 87–90, 93, 94, 96, 97
monetary policy 65, 182, 183
Moody's 186
municipal (muni) bond market 48

N

NASD Bondinfo 182
negative convexity 98
net cost of carry 110, 111, 113
net price 32, 33, 46, 53
Nigel Webb Software 123, 134, 135, 141, 142, 144, 187
nominal value 9, 18, 38, 41, 53

O

Optimum 187
option brokers 152
option premium 146–148, 150–152
option writers 118, 132, 139
option-valuation model 104, 119, 130, 133, 140, 177
Osaka Futures Exchange 189
'out of the money' 103, 125

P

panic 157
par value 18, 19, 26, 29, 32, 36–38, 44, 51, 53
parity 86, 151, 176, 177, 179, 189

payback period 161, 163, 166, 167
portfolio duration 80
present value 12–14, 31, 79, 81
principal 4, 7–10, 13–17, 41, 42, 50, 52, 53, 55, 66, 79, 81, 82
put–call ratio 154
puttable bonds 48

R

rating agencies 185
redemption yields 4, 33, 35, 45, 47, 63, 64, 66, 68, 69, 71, 73, 92
Reuters 98
rho 138, 141, 142
risk of default 36, 66
risk premium 58
risk-free rate of return 14, 36, 66, 79, 118–120, 122, 132, 133, 139
RiskGrades 186
RPI 4, 17, 50, 51, 53–56
RPI adjustment basis 53, 54
running yield 4, 25–31, 33

S

Saks Inc. 2% Convertible 2024 167
SEC filing 165
SEK HK$ Zero-coupon Bond Due 2018 40
sensitivity of a bond portfolio 75
SG Warrants 189, 190
shares 3, 13, 19, 103, 106, 109, 122, 123, 126, 136, 145–148, 152, 161, 163–167, 171, 176, 180, 188
simple yield 25
single stock futures 112
spread 5, 17, 36, 50, 51, 62–67, 87, 98, 104, 162
Standard and Poors 186
standard deviation 105, 106, 108
static return 146, 150, 151
stock market indices 103
strip (and strippable bonds) 40, 41

T

theta 138, 141, 142
time to maturity 38, 42, 68, 73, 78, 79

time value   12, 72, 73, 103, 125, 127–129, 132, 139, 141, 179
time value of an option   125
'time value of money' theory   12, 72
Tokyo International Financial Futures Exchange   189
trade settlement date   18, 19, 21
TradingLab   190
traditional warrants   161, 169, 172, 174, 175, 190

U

UK 5% Treasury stock 2008   28
UK gilts yield curve   80, 181
UK government securities ('gilts')   73
UK Treasury 8% 2015   28
'underlying'   24, 103, 104, 110–120, 122–136, 139–143, 145–148, 151, 152, 154, 161–165, 168–171, 174–177, 179, 188
US 2% Treasury 10-year Inflation-Indexed Note 2014   56
US Bond Market Association   182
US Treasury Note   2014 34, 35

V

vega   138, 141, 142

volatility   73, 103–109, 116, 118–123, 128, 130, 132–135, 138–143, 152, 175, 186

W

Wall Street Journal   21, 186
Wal-Mart 6.875% 2009   90, 97
warrant delta   177, 179
warrant price   151, 162, 169–173, 176, 177, 179, 190
worst-case yield   44

Y

yield curve   35, 62, 68–71, 73, 74, 92
yield spreads   62–66
yield to maturity (YTM)   30, 31, 36, 37, 46, 47, 68, 75–78, 81, 84, 85, 88–90, 92, 94, 96, 97
yield to next call   48
yield to refunding   48
yield to worst   44–48

Z

zero-coupon bond   17, 37–42, 50, 79, 94, 98

Magic Numbers
The 33 Key Ratios That Every Investor Should Know
Peter Temple

Written by a leading finance expert, this book offers readers simple explanations on how to calculate and interpret key financial ratios- information that is essential for the accurate assessment of a company's financial condition and the true value of its shares. This comprehensive resource is packed with numerous examples from actual company reports and features a supporting Web site at www.magicnumbersbook.com. Readers will also find many online reference sources, including company Web sites and free software offers.

With a focus on private investors and written in an accessible manner, this book not only covers the range of ratios that would benefit investors involving in bonds, futures and options but offers valuable information that can be applied universally. There are very few books that have explored this topic in such an easy-to-read manner.

0-471-47924-1 • Cloth • 228 pages • October 2001

Magic Numbers for Stock Investors
How To Calculate The 25 Key Ratios For Investing Success
Peter Temple

Building on the success of the original *Magic Numbers* and using wholly new and up to date examples, **Magic Numbers for Stock Investors** looks at key ratios that all investors can use easily to look at the financial health and growth prospects of a company before they buy shares in it. The ratios are described in details, with simple formulas, and help on where to find the data needed to calculate them. There are worked examples, both fictional and actual, in each 'magic number' section.

The book follows the same format of *Magic Numbers* (published 2002). But the difference is that it focuses specifically on ratios that are of use to investors in shares. All examples are new and fully updated; around a dozen new ratios have been added; and all worked company examples are different to those in the original book.

0-470-82124-8 • Cloth • 212 pages • October 2003

FORTHCOMING TITLES

Magic Numbers for Human Resource Management
Hugh Bucknall - Mercer
0-470-82161-2 • Cloth • 250 pages

Magic Numbers for Consumer Marketing
John Davis
0-470-82162-0 • Cloth • 228 pages